ON FLY-FISHING
THE BEAR RIVER WATERSHED

ESSAYS AND EXCEPTIONAL
MISADVENTURES

CHADD VANZANTEN

THE
History
PRESS

Published by The History Press
Charleston, SC
www.historypress.com

All photos and images were produced by the author, except where otherwise noted.

First published 2021

Manufactured in the United States

ISBN 9781467149099

Library of Congress Control Number: 2020951820

For Amanda

CONTENTS

ACKNOWLEDGEMENTS

This book exists only because of the generosity and accommodation of my family, friends and various experts.

Thank you, experts, Frank Amato, Chris Barkey, Phaedra Budy, Star Coulbrooke, Lynn de Freitas, Emily Lewis, Darren Parry and Mark Vinson, for your knowledge and insight. Thanks to my fishing pals for agreeing (if not willingly, at least tacitly) to be characters in this book—Andrew, Bill, Donicio, Jason, Paul, Russ, Tim, Tim and Tyler. A few of you functioned as consultant *and* literary character—thank you, Jim, Brad, Matt and Ken.

Most of my artistic undertakings are still in some way intended to convince my children that I'm good at something, so for their continued tolerance, I thank Shreve, Klaus, Ingrid and Gretchen. Thank you, Pete at *Fly Culture*, for aiding and abetting my writing habit. Thanks to my writing group, and special thanks to my writing mentors—Jay, Sandra and Star.

Thank you, Andrew, Bill, Erin, Jesse, Klaus, Kyle and Tyler, for your abnormally excellent photography. Thanks, Artie, for your unflagging patience and support.

Deep and loving gratitude to Amanda—wife, partner, friend and muse.

Please visit:

facebook.com/onflyfishing
thecolemancollection.org
@thecolemancollection
@backwaterflyfishing
flydudesguiding.com

reeldealanglers.com
flyculturemag.com
@bradphansen
@Donicio71

Bear River, 1905. *Courtesy of USU Special Collections, Merrill-Cazier Library.*

BEAR RIVER WATERSHED
HISTORICAL TIMELINE

1,000,000 years ago	Bear River Mountains form
250,000 years ago	Bear Lake forms
140,000 years ago	Volcanic eruptions at Soda Point redirect Bear River
14,000 years ago	Lake Bonneville drains
12,500 years ago	Paleo-Indian cultures inhabit Bear River watershed
11,000 years ago	Sediment dam separates Bear River and Bear Lake
AD 1	Fremont culture inhabits Bear River watershed
1300	Shoshone people inhabit Bear River watershed
1805	Shoshone people encounter Lewis and Clark
1812	American Fur Company trappers name the Bear River "Miller River"
1818	Northwest Fur Company trappers give the Bear River present name

1822	Northwestern Shoshone chief Sagwitch Timbimboo is born
1852	Mormon settlers arrive in Cache Valley
1862	"First" water right claim on Bear River by Myers Ranch (Wyoming)
January 29, 1863	Massacre at Boa Ogoi (Bear River Massacre)
1869	Transcontinental Railroad complete
1871	James M. Keller Sr. settles in Mink Creek
1883	Brown trout introduced in United States
March 20, 1887	Sagwitch Timbimboo dies
1889	Wheelon Dam completed (first dam on Bear River)
July 3 and 10, 1890	Idaho and Wyoming granted U.S. statehood
1890s–early 1900s	Brown trout introduced in Bear River watershed
January 4, 1896	Utah granted U.S. statehood
1911	Bear River diverted into Bear Lake
1917	Cove Dam completed
1918	Stewart Dam completed
1923	Frank Clark kills Old Ephraim
1927	James Needham salmonfly collection (earliest known in Logan River)
1958	Bear River Compact signed by President Dwight D. Eisenhower
1966	Nancy Erman salmonfly collection (last known in Logan River)
1978	*Curtis Creek Manifesto* by Sheridan Anderson published

1980	Amended Bear River Compact signed by President Jimmy Carter
1983	Severe flooding in Utah; Bear River peaks at 9,750 cubic feet per second
1984	High Uintas Wilderness Area established
March 31, 1984	Sheridan Anderson dies
1986	Bear Lake reaches full-pool elevation (5,923.65 feet)
1991	Bear River Development Act signed into law
1994	Absence of salmonflies in Logan River discovered by USU Bug Lab
June 4, 2000	Jodi and Kevin Conatser cited for criminal trespass on Weber River
2001	Mark Vinson's first Logan River salmonfly experiments
2003	Right Fork Project begins
2004	Salmonfly transplants initiated in Logan River
2005	Evidence of transplanted salmonflies found in Logan River
2006	Benson Road illegally closed
September 2006	Cove Dam removed
December 2006	Twin Lakes Canal Company files Federal Energy Regulatory Commission pre-application for new dam construction
March 2007	TLCC files water-right application for new dam construction
2008	Mark Vinson leaves USU Bug Lab; salmonfly transplants discontinued
April 2008	Utah Supreme Court decision in *Conatser v. Johnson*
2009	Brown trout removed from Right Fork

May 2010	Public Waters Access Act signed into law
November 2010	*USAC v. VR Acquisitions*
May 2011	*USAC v. Orange Street Development*
2012	Right Fork fish-passage barrier installed
July 2012	TLCC water-right application denied
2013	Right Fork stocked with Bonneville cutthroat
April 11, 2014	Leness Keller dies
July 2015	Final (?) Benson Road closure petition denied
June 2016	TLCC dam construction FERC application rejected
November 2017	Utah Supreme Court decision in *USAC v. Orange Street Development*
2018	Utah Division of Water Resources files Bear Lake water claim
February 2019	Utah Supreme Court remands *USAC v. VR Acquisitions*
January 2020	Groundbreaking for new Boa Ogoi memorial site

I

A POWERFUL DRY

By the time we finished the hike and shuffled into the trailhead parking lot, I was working on a powerful dry.

A little water sloshed around in my water bottle, but I didn't want that. It had been clear and cold when I filtered it from a trailside stream a couple hours earlier, but it'd since turned tepid and plasticky tasting, the bottle itself reesty from five days of backwash. The hike was done, and I was done with the water bottle. I wanted a vodka tonic. Or just iced tea, but at least iced water from some municipally approved culinary water source.

And I wanted it in a goddamn glass.

It was my fishing buddy Tim King who coined the term "powerful dry." After a hot day or long drive, he'd say, "Let's grab a beer. I got a powerful dry."

"Good name for a fly pattern," I'd once told him.

Tim was bearded and barrel chested, built like a recently retired lumberjack, but in fact, he had just retired from a government job building rocket motors for the space shuttle. About all he did now was play amateur hockey and take fly-fishing trips like the one we'd just finished, but he also salvaged and restored discarded things to their former beauty and utility— old Coleman lanterns, vintage Volkswagens, busted bamboo flyrods. He'd been restoring one such rod for me, but it wasn't ready in time for this trip.

At the trailhead, Russ Beck unlocked his car and raised the hatchback. Tall and wookiee-like, Russ was one of my first fishing buddies. The three of us shrugged off our backpacks, exhaling with profound relief.

Bear River at Christmas Meadows, 1869. *Courtesy of U.S. Library of Congress.*

Tim said to me, "You sit in the front seat this time—I'm gonna crawl inna back and go to sleep."

"I might need to do that, too," said Russ, dropping into the driver's seat.

We're not backpackers. We're anglers with backpacks. There's a big difference. For starters, we get winded way more easily than backpackers. Moreover, for some reason, backpackers want to hike farther, longer. Anglers only want the most impressive fish-to-mile ratio attainable. So, while backpackers rack up trail miles, anglers prefer to rack them *down*. And in this case, the Forest Service had evidently rerouted the Middle Basin trail recently, making our hike considerably longer than shown on our maps, which was not appreciated.

"No way that was seven miles," I complained. The car doors thunked shut. I asked Russ, "How far does your step-counter watch thingy say we hiked today?"

He tapped the gizmo on his wrist and answered, "Nine and a half."

"I believe it," protested Tim from the back seat. "I'm beat."

The bellyaching wasn't an act, but it wasn't exactly genuine, either. It was a way to behave at the end of the trail, an agreed-to attitude we'd adopted.

Others at the trailhead were doing little high-fives and validating each other's feelings; Tim and Russ and I acted self-righteously pooped, maybe to reassure ourselves that the hike was actually worth grumbling about.

We were footsore and dry, but we'd gotten what we'd come for. There were scores of hand-sized brook trout, a smaller number of two-pound tiger trout and some pretty little cutthroats. The viewscapes were predictably impressive. We laughed and drank whiskey around the campfire every night. And the challenge was perfect—strenuous enough for us to credibly bitch about when we were back home without having inflicted any lasting physical harm to ourselves.

I turned to Tim in the back seat and said, "Great trip, though."

"Oh, yeah, yeah," Tim admitted, perking up. "Fantastic." And then, stricken again: "But, man, am I beat."

I'd come to the Uintas to fish and take in the grandeur, but I'd also come to investigate the headwaters of the Bear River. At the risk of sounding trite, I'd come to *meet* the upper reaches of the watershed where I learned pretty much everything I know about fly-fishing.

I fish the Bear River whenever I can, but there is a limited number of publicly accessible sections of the mainstem where a fly-angler can catch a decent fish. Much of the Bear runs through private property, and much of it does not support trout. So, I fish the Bear's tributaries—the Logan River, Little Bear River, Blacksmith Fork, Cub River—more often. These streams

McPheters Lake, Uinta Mountains.

taught me to fly-fish. And although the Bear River headwaters lie only a few hours from where I live, I'd never been there. To crib from John Denver, I was returning to a place I'd never been before.

On the first day of the trip, as soon as we got out of the car, I felt a strange energy. I couldn't characterize it, but I felt something, so I leaned into the hike, eager to reach the source.

The Bear River rises from the north slope of the Uinta Mountains in Summit County, Utah, at the inside corner of the trademark notch in the state's otherwise quadrate boundary. In strict geographical terms, the Bear River begins at the confluence of Hayden Fork and Stillwater Fork, near Christmas Meadows, just within the Uinta-Wasatch-Cache National Forest, at an elevation of 8,510 feet.

In freer terms, however, the headwaters comprise five basins at twelve thousand feet elevation and higher in the High Uinta Wilderness Area. From there, the Bear heads north into Wyoming and flows along its western border. Then it swerves into Idaho and makes a grand arrowhead-shaped turn around the northern end of the Bear River Mountains and back toward Utah.

During this circuitous 350-mile odyssey, the Bear sheds elevation rapidly. By the time it hits Evanston, Wyoming, less than thirty miles from the Uintas, the elevation is 6,749 feet. That's a drop of 1,700 feet from the Stillwater-Hayden confluence, but it's a plummet of over 5,000 feet from the High Uinta headwater basins. With over 300 miles of its total extent still ahead of it, the Bear has lost two thirds of its elevation. The river will drop only another 2,500 feet before emptying into Great Salt Lake at around 4,200 feet—just 85 miles from its own headwaters.

An aerial view of the headwater basins resembles a colossal oak leaf, each basin a lobe of the leaf and each stream a vein converging at the leaf's midrib. Working clockwise from east to west, they are Amethyst Basin, Middle Basin, West Basin, Hell Hole Basin and Hayden Canyon. Here snowmelt and stormwater accumulate drop by drop to become the Bear River.

There is a lot of water up there.

You can see it seeping from the mountains as though they're towering leaky old casks. Hayden Peak and nearby Mount Agassiz weep dark stripes down their pinkish-cream-colored quartzite faces. The Uintas also give rise to the Provo, Weber and Duchesne Rivers.

You can see the water in ubiquitous trickles that crisscross the alpine meadows. They're too small to have names, too small even to know how to refer to them—runnels? Streamlets? Their flows range from that of a

Ryder Lake, Uinta Mountains, 1869. *Courtesy of U.S. Library of Congress.*

garden hose up to what you might call a creek if it held even a single fish. Everywhere you go, you hear flowing water. On the trails, you must hop over or slog through these—runlets—and the countless boggy spots they create.

"Goddam little rivulets keep cutting across the trail," Tim grumbled as we hopscotched wearily from rock to rock across yet another mud hole.

"Yeah," I said, "they really slow you down, don't they?"

"They're killin' me."

You can't see the water in the ground, but you can detect it underfoot. Even in mid-August, the earth is dark and damp and sometimes vaguely springy. After only an hour of rainfall, clear water runs in sheets over the peaty soil.

You can, of course, see the water in the ponds and lakes. In Middle Basin, McPheters Lake covers almost thirty acres; Ryder Lake covers thirteen. The basin is also dotted by three dozen ponds, which, along with the lakes, give rise to Stillwater Fork, the larger of the Bear's two headwater tributaries.

Hayden Fork, the smaller tributary, is not fed by lakes but runs down from the north slopes of Hayden Peak. As the Bear River flows out of the Uintas,

Tim King.

its annual average discharge is around two hundred cubic feet per second. This will double and triple in about a hundred miles.

There is a lot of water up there, but the Bear soon enters very thirsty country. Utah, for example, is the second-most arid state in the Union, but its per-capita daily water use is over 180 gallons, higher than states that are not nearly as arid.

The Bear River flows through a powerful dry. And it shows. The Bear has been dammed and divvied up in the 130 years since its first water development, now impounded behind seven major mainstem dams and checked by dozens of other diversions. Grace Dam in Idaho diverts the entire river from its course for use at a hydroelectric plant five miles away. In the 1890s, the Bear River's flow was rather brutishly rerouted into and back out of Bear Lake to store yet more of its water.

More than two million people in three states rely on Bear River water for agriculture, drinking water and electricity. Ten million migratory birds depend quite urgently on Great Salt Lake, which receives 60 percent of its inflow from the Bear. Before European settlement, the Bear probably thundered along at ten thousand cubic feet per second; today, there are sections you can cross without really getting wet, and the section between the Bear Lake inlet and outlet canals is effectively dewatered. And yet, the Bear is still the largest river in the United States that does not drain into any ocean, and there is almost always talk of constructing more dams here.

There is a lot of water up there, but it will never be enough.

There are also a lot of people up there. A knife-edge ridgeline encircles Middle Basin, connecting a chain of pyramidal Precambrian peaks and walling off the area like the mountain sanctuary of kung fu mystics. As darkness fell on our camp each night, we certainly felt isolated. There were no sights or sounds of permanent civilization, and the sky was wilderness black, despite the Klieg-like waxing moon.

And yet there were dozens of other campers around—three camps on our side of McPheters Lake and more on the far side. Most groups were just two or three people, but there was a Boy Scout troop of eleven out there somewhere—we heard them hooting and shouting after dark.

One night, Tim and I left our firepit and walked in the darkness down to McPheters Lake to collect water. There was no wind, so the reflected light of campfires and headlamps on the opposite shore glimmered festively on the lake's glassy face.

"It looks like there's a resort over there," I said, kneeling with my bottle and water filter. "Looks like a garden party over there."

"I was just thinking that," said Tim, looking across the lake. The sound of laughter drifted over to us. "Maybe if we hurry," he sneered, "we can make it there in time for backgammon."

Across the West, more people are availing themselves of public lands. Backcountry recreation—once the avocation of hardcore hikers, hippies and crusty hermitic anglers—is now unquestionably mainstream. Public lands are being inexorably loved to death. One imagines a future in which we retreat to vacant cities to escape the crowds and clamor of the wilderness.

I might be overstating the case.

In truth, Middle Basin is two miles wide and three miles long, and we shared it with about fifty other backpackers, none of whom camped anywhere near us. Conditions weren't exactly cramped, but the expectation of total solitude in a federally designated wilderness, although no longer realistic, is still very much alive.

So, we smiled tartly at the others we encountered, our annoyance never altogether concealed, but it was like pointing an accusing finger at a mirror— the noisy assholes across the lake were scoffing right back at us.

We had McPheters Lake to ourselves each morning when we fished there for brook trout. Most were undistinguished in terms of size, but Russ and Tim caught a few that were over twelve inches. On the second day, we strung nine or ten little brookies on a tree branch. We wrapped them in foil that night, roasted them by the fire and made fish tacos with corn tortillas and limes.

On the final full day of the trip, Russ and I hiked up to Ryder Lake, which is said to hold big tiger trout. The lake perches on a rocky shelf overlooking McPheters, guarded by rocky cliffs that stand crumbling like the bastions of old castles. We inched along the shoreline, casting to a few risers, but the wind was high, and we caught no fish.

By midday, rain clouds formed along Middle Basin's lofty southern rim. Every twenty minutes or so, a new cloud would roil up on the ridgeline, hang there gray and damp for a few minutes as if snagged on the rock and then separate suddenly and join others gliding away in a line that advanced northward on the wind.

"I think I'm gonna head back," reported Russ, reeling in his line. He frowned at the sky. "I don't wanna get rained on."

"I'm gonna hang out for a while," I replied, "hike around, see if the fishing will turn on."

I hiked uphill until there was nothing above me but scree fields and the uppermost mountain slopes, which encircled the valley like a great amphitheater carpeted in lawns of forbs and wildflowers. Beneath me were the lakes and ponds of Middle Basin.

The ground was just as soggy up there, so I sat on a table of sun-warmed rock and ate my lunch, trying again to name the energy I'd felt the day we arrived. But it wasn't so simple. This wasn't just a blissed-out Rocky Mountain high. It was something complicated and restless, something emitting from me.

Ryder Lake tiger trout. *Courtesy of Erin Reed.*

Another cloud appeared at the ridgeline, lingered and then detached abruptly, like a soap bubble blown trembling from a toy bubble wand. It peppered the mountainside with a spiteful little volley of rain. I pulled on my rain jacket and surveyed the valley in the flattened light. I couldn't see all the way back to Christmas Meadows, but I saw the Uintas marching to the Utah border in great folds of terrain. Beyond that was Wyoming and the inference of Idaho.

Soon the sun shone again and resolved smaller details. Furtive marmots darting through quartzite escarpments. Birds of prey circling. Rise-rings way down on McPheters.

And people. Most were mere specks to me, but their neon-colored gear caught my eye—a cluster of fluorescent tents nestled in a squat spruce copse, a file of hikers threading down a trail. A group of seven young people and several adults gathered at the shore of Ryder, not far from where I'd been fishing with Russ a couple hours before. I heard them hollering.

Ah, I thought, that's the damn Boy Scout troop.

Uncertainty—that was the energy I'd felt. A current of uncertainty and scarcity ran down Middle Basin, into the Bear River and out into the vast and powerful dry beyond. But it wasn't a force that existed there; it was my own anxiety about the extreme pressure that ranchers, farmers, Boy Scouts and all the rest of us exert on the watershed.

And it wasn't just water. It was animals, too, and plants. Fully half of the trees in Middle Basin stood dead and gray, likely the result of invasive pine beetle infestations, sponsored in part by climate change. I hadn't seen any bears or pikas. Ryder Lake held no native cutthroat; it was stocked instead with tiger trout, a laboratory fish. McPheters held brook trout, unevictable holdovers from times past when fecund nonnatives were employed as planters. Even the small cutthroats I'd hooked down in Hayden Creek on our first day were agency-stocked, probably via airdrop.

Uncertainty—how long before places like this no longer exist?

I went down to Ryder Lake at dusk to try again for fish. The wind was flagging, blustering in gusts. When the water stilled, it was easier to spot the tigers patrolling, rising, boiling.

Bright orange, size 6, tungsten-head streamer: refused.

Bright green, size 8, foam hopper: refused.

Bright red, size 10 Stimulator: refused.

Dull gray, size 12 Bird Nest: bingo.

I'd cadged the Bird Nest off Tim. It's a wet fly pattern that offhandedly imitates whatever aquatic insect happens to be emerging at the moment. It is perhaps the most flamboyantly nondescript fly pattern I've ever seen, like a guy on a street corner wearing an overcoat and fake plastic nose with spectacles, pretending to read a newspaper. The only thing this fly didn't do was whistle nonchalantly. And it worked. Like many backcountry lakes, McPheters had a line of foam that gyred slowly past the banks in the counterclockwise direction. I put the Bird Nest in the foam and hooked four tigers ranging in size from fourteen to eighteen inches.

I got back to camp just before dark. We were quiet around the campfire that night. It's always quiet on the last night. We'd planned for an optional sixth day, but neither Tim nor Russ mentioned it. I had enough food for an extra day but only enough whiskey for one more hot toddy, so I stayed quiet, too. I made my toddy, and we shared the trip's final toast.

The next day, on the hike out, one of the big gray clouds swooped down, parked and released a payload of heavy rain. Puddles formed on the trail at once, and the forest steamed and dripped like a jungle. Then the squall gathered strength, and a hard wind blew. The trees deflected unnervingly above us, moaning and creaking like a fleet of moored-up wooden ships.

At last, we reached the car, and I got in the front passenger seat with the reesty water in my bottle. We drove north out of the mountains and stopped at the Bear River Ranger Station. Under the disapproving gaze of youthful Forest Service agents, we snuck one by one into the public restroom, stripped to the waist, and washed up in the sink. Then we continued north on Mirror Lake Highway, catching glimpses of the Bear River winding through subalpine aspen forests.

"That looks glorious," exclaimed Russ, pointing through the windshield. "Why the hell did we hike ten miles into the mountains? Why aren't we just fishing *that*?"

But then we exited the national forest, and the river was enclosed by barbed wire fencing stretched tight between brawny wooden posts. Hanging from the wire with a frequency that struck me as vindictive were loudly lettered private property signs.

"There's just that short stretch of public water there," I explained.

Some miles later, another stunning section of the river hove into view, with bends and pools lined with spruce and shimmering aspen, but this, too, was fenced and conspicuously posted. It was a sprawling private development of palatial riverside McMansions.

"From here on out it's mostly private 'til you get to Evanston," I said. "Bear River State Park. It's got exactly one-point-five miles of publicly accessible river."

Soon the Bear broke west, meandering out of view and through private ranches and estates, but the feeling of scarcity lingered. We drove north through the rolling ag lands and pastures dotted with hundreds of corpulent black angus cattle. All of this was watered by the Bear River watershed—crops, pastures, cattle, houses. When we settled around a table in the Painted Lady Saloon in Evanston and our server greeted us with pilsner glasses of ice water, we were drinking from the Bear then, too.

Compared to its pre-settlement condition, the Bear River is a phantom of its former self. A century and a half of overuse has left the watershed and ecosystem gasping for life. Of the more than sixty tributaries in the watershed, fifty-two are classified as impaired by agriculture-related pollution and water quality issues. The watershed's native trout species, the Bonneville cutthroat, balances on the edge of extirpation. Other species—from June bugs to grizzly bears—have disappeared from areas where they were once abundant.

At Great Salt Lake, water levels are within a foot of historic disastrous low points. Antelope Island is now a peninsula; the bison that inhabit it might soon be able to wander to nearby Salt Lake International Airport over dry ground. Even the humans are getting concerned—these declines could cost Utah more than $1 billion in various derivative revenue from brine shrimp harvest and mineral extraction. There is even speculation that the cobalt and arsenic in the desiccated lakebed will become a toxic windborne plume of fallout that showers periodically onto the densely populated Salt Lake Valley.

Here again, I might be overstating things.

It's difficult to avoid looking back in anger. In truth, the news isn't all bad. For instance, conservation organizations like Trout Unlimited work constantly with farmers and ranchers in the watershed to reverse the negative effects of historic water development. They screen irrigation diversions to prevent fish from swimming into ag fields, and they reconnect tributaries that have been severed from the Bear River—in some cases for more than a century.

Similarly, fish researchers are quietly restoring Bonneville cutthroat trout to the watershed, working on one small tributary at a time to create tiny strongholds where native cutthroats can spawn and recruit without the deadly interdiction of nonnative brown trout. From California to Colorado, cutthroats are returning a handful at a time to their native waterways.

In February 2019, the Utah State Senate passed a resolution that might finally allow water users to implement a form of "water banking," thereby circumventing the archaic and perverse use-it-or-lose-it stipulation of western water law, which in effect encourages water users in arid states to be needlessly profligate. For the first time in history, water users might be able to leave their water in streams without compromising their claims and rights.

Closer to my home, the City of Logan, Utah, has formed a task force to restore urbanized sections of the Logan River, the Bear River's largest tributary. The city has spent $2 million on channel realignment, floodplain restoration, and reintroduction of riverside native plant species—and there are proposals to spend that much again on further improvements.

And although the 1991 Bear River Development Act directed the Utah Division of Water Rights to build more dams in the Bear River Valley, no new dams have been built in the three decades since. One dam has even been *removed*. This is partially due to vigorous public opposition to the appalling environmental costs associated with dams, but it's also because Utah is finally learning to use its water efficiently, so the water that a new dam would provide isn't yet critically needed.

So, perhaps my vision of dazed, dusty buffalo and gaunt survivors in gasmasks wandering together through a withered urban hellscape in search of water is more of a worst-case scenario.

A week after the Uintas trip, Tim gave me the bamboo flyrod he'd been rehabilitating, a two-piece Tonka Prince originally manufactured by Horrock-Ibbotson of Utica, New York, in the 1950s. Tim had wrapped on new guides, replaced the handle and reel seat and re-lacquered the bamboo.

We went outside to cast it. It was a hot day in August. The rod shone in the sun like some ancient golden artifact. The action was not exactly slow—more like dreamy. At first, I whip-cracked the backcast and couldn't get a loop to form.

"Let the rod do the work," Tim advised. "You don't hafta force it."

I eased up and was able to cast one good loop and then another, and soon, the fly was landing more or less where I told it to.

"There ya go," said Tim. "Slow everything down. It's like stepping backward in time."

I took the flyrod to a small, lesser-known Bear River tributary, the upper reach of which is largely unmarred by development or overuse. Up there,

Bear River Bonneville cutthroat trout.

I didn't feel bothered by the cattle and crops guzzling the Bear River like a cold beer. In fact, there were thunderstorms. The powerful dry seemed far away, and the anxiety I'd felt in the Uintas began to dissipate.

I moved upstream and cast the old Tonka Prince, probably more carefully than necessary, laying dry flies on the narrow tongues of current that raced between cobbles, casting to the secret, upwelling pillows beneath the woody bankside vegetation. It was a marvel of engineering, the little flyrod, and Tim had resurrected it to an exquisite state. It was certainly a better rod now than it had been in its original instantiation, but more astonishing was that it could be restored at all, around seventy years old and constructed essentially of grass.

On that stream, the cutthroat population is natural and self-sustaining and a few of them can grow to eighteen inches. The best tactic is to move up the center of the channel slowly, hoping to stalk up behind actively feeding trout. It's not uncommon to spot and hook them only six feet upstream.

So, that's what I did. I waded up the center, and I spotted an active cutthroat and hooked him in just ten inches of water ten feet ahead of me. When I'd let him go, I spotted another, so I hooked him, too.

And it went on like that for a while.

2

IN THE SHOULDER SEASONS

During my entire first year of fly-fishing, I fished alone. It wasn't because I'm introverted or snobby—kind of the opposite, actually. It was because no one wants to fish with the rookie. Rookies are slow. They get underfoot. They ask lots of questions—like a kid asking where babies come from. It's unfair but true: rookies are the worst. At first even I was ambivalent about fishing with me.

But, eventually, I didn't mind it at all. Fishing alone allowed me to take my time, make stupid mistakes in private, and figure out on my own where babies come from.

Nevertheless, I worked on my cast, haunted the local fly shop and poked my head into a few Trout Unlimited meetings—just in case. After another year, I began to meet what are known as fishing buddies.

And I didn't like any of them.

One way to quickly locate new fishing buddies is to take your flyrod out onto your front lawn and throw a couple casts. Fly anglers from all over will show up to give you advice.

"Drop your elbow," they'll say. "Slow down."

By employing this technique, I discovered a neighbor of mine was secretly a fly angler. My tailing loop apparently offended him at a range of several hundred yards.

"You're overloading the rod on the forward," he explained, pantomiming while still crossing the street. "You gotta come forward steadily."

"How long you been fishing?" I asked.

He shrugged a smug little shrug. "I know what I'm doing." He told me to drop my elbow and slow down.

When he turned to go, I asked, "Hey, you wanna fish on Saturday? Hit the Blacksmith Fork?"

I think he wanted to decline but was taken off guard, so he mumbled, "Yeah, okay. I guess."

On the appointed afternoon, he stopped by and asked, "Is it all right if we drive separately?"

"Sure," I answered. "Where should we meet?"

"Ah, we don't have to meet," he said as he went back across the street. "Just go where you want to fish, and I'll go where I want."

Damn, I thought, he really does know what he's doing.

That winter I fished with a young guy who had lots of boutique gear and designer outdoor duds. He used nicknames for all the famous rivers (the Galley, the Maddy, the Mo'), as though he fished them so frequently that he couldn't be bothered to say their proper names every single time. This led me to believe he, too, knew what he was doing, but after we'd dead-drifted nymphs on the Logan for two hours without hooking a single fish, I realized he knew even less than I did—a distinction belonging to a very limited few. But I didn't mind his lack of experience. It was the macho, the gonzo, the aggro that bothered me, talking about "rippin' lips" and "slayin' hogs," then sulking when there were no hogs to slay or lips to rip.

Lots of the anglers I met acted that way—bragging, gloating, sulking, posing. And, my god, the temper tantrums. I appreciated the occasional profane rant, but a grown man apoplectic over a treed fly felt unseemly and impure. I rarely fished with anyone more than once or twice.

Maybe it was me. Maybe I was the ragey weirdo who gloated and sulked. Either way, I soon reverted to solo fishing, and I'd been doing fine that way for several years when I met Russ Beck and Brad Hansen.

I met Russ at an open mic reading at a little tea house in town. He was writing narrative nonfiction about his Mormon faith crisis. I was writing short fiction about mine. Neither of us had written about fly-fishing—Russ didn't know how to fish, and I didn't know how to write—but within five years, we'd write a whole book on fly-fishing together.

A few years later, we met Brad. He was married to my coworker Janelle. She thought Brad fished too often, and she'd heard me complain about fishing too little, so she introduced me to Brad thinking that my fishing schedule would hamper Brad's, and his schedule would improve mine. This didn't pan out—Brad and I both fished more often after that.

Still, I was wary about rebounding into any new fly-fishing relationships. Brad and Russ seemed like good guys, but how would they act after four hours of mediocre fishing? Or four hours of fantastic fishing? Would it be them who found me insufferable? Fly-fishing exposes either your best or worst because your streamside behavior eventually reveals that of your everyday life. You can hide yourself from the fish, but you can't hide from the fishing.

Brad was what I considered a "serious angler." On the water he was cunning and relentless, a grad student in environmental history who traded his hard-earned free time for captured fish at the most favorable exchange rates possible. I never once saw him encroach water he hadn't already ruthlessly fished out, and he roved around the river to line up the best shots, like a pro pool shark studying a billiards table. Brad would back away from a promising riffle, cross to the opposite bank twenty yards downriver and then come up the other side for an only slightly better spot to cast.

He was a numbers man, too—he wanted bigger fish and more of them. He kept score, but I never considered him a score*keeper*, and the idea of Brad ever gloating was absurd. When he'd occasionally lose a big fish, he'd laugh it off and then forget it. And he'd laugh his ass off when Russ or I lost big fish, but somehow, this made us feel better, not worse.

Most importantly, Brad fished by a code. He fished as deliberately and effectively as possible, and although he was never a dick about it, he expected Russ and me to do likewise.

Missouri River, Montana.

"Someone gonna fish that stretch right there?" he'd reprove, pointing his rod at a favorable but brush-screened run that we'd skipped. "There's fish in there."

Russ or I would sigh and say, "Yeah, I'll do it," knowing we'd just end up snagged.

And Brad would laugh. "Hey, I'll do it if no one else will, but someone should."

"Yeah."

At first, I figured Russ wouldn't like fishing with Brad. Because if Brad's fishing style was all business, Russ's was no business. No structure, no expectations. Russ was an unfussy angler, a wandering angler, choosing his shot based not on how productive it might be but on how unlikely it was to result in a snag. When we fished in the summertime, Russ often disappeared for an hour to nap on the riverbank. He loved catching a good fish, but his ultimate objective was to be an angler, so he succeeded every single time he went fishing.

My philosophy fell someplace between theirs—fussier than Russ but less disciplined than Brad. I'd been fishing the longest, so I had a few things to teach them both, but somehow, I had less patience than either.

Maybe it was our dissimilarities that made us a good team—we each had our place on a continuum. There was even a certain pleasing variety in our collective physical appearances—Brad is of medium height and wiry; Russ is tall, shaggy, imposing; and I fall between the two, taller and much bulkier than Brad but smaller than Russ.

Moreover, none of us were overly fond of the macho-aggro fly-fishing culture that was emerging back then and is now well established. We weren't after hogs or toads or lips to rip. I think we agreed that fish were a pretty great natural resource but that we should pay due respect. To this day, Russ apologizes to practically every fish he catches.

"Sorry, sir," he says to the fish, quite without irony. "Let's get you back in the water—just hold still a sec—sorry. There. Go on home. Thank you."

The three of us began fishing together a couple times a month and sometimes every weekend. We fished solo and with others, too, but the assumption was that we'd fish together if possible, making other arrangements only if one of us couldn't make it, and for about three years, this was our default fishing configuration. Blacksmith Fork, Right Fork, Left Fork, Logan River, Bear River, Little Bear River, Cub River, Cinnamon Creek, Rock Creek, Curtis Creek—for three years and through all four seasons, we fished the Bear River watershed in this three-man team.

The typical outing began with Russ. His schedule was the tightest, so he was always updating us with bulletins about his free time.

"I'm free after 4:00 today," Russ would text. "I need to fish. Run up Blacksmith Fork after work? Or Wednesday?"

Sometimes his texts hinted at grander ambitions: "I'm clear for Saturday. We should hit the Narrows in the morning and then Black Canyon? I'm clear for all day."

Brad fished the most (still does), so he'd turn the concept into a plan. He'd run the time of day, season and his own most recent fishing success through his internal fishing algorithm and make a suggestion: "Black Canyon is crowded lately. Let's do Last Chance."

We had names for the places we fished—Last Chance, the Squatch, the Real Shitty Place.

The day and time set, a few logistical texts might be in order.

"I was gonna tie some zebra midges but I forgot. Anyone have some?"

"I have some."

"Make it 1:30? My kid's got a thing."

"Sure."

Russ and I were usually content with fishing places where we knew we'd catch fish, but Brad disdained routine and brought us to untested waters, even when it involved a high probability of getting skunked.

"Got a new place I want to take you fellows. Bring plenty of nymphs. Dress warm. See you in the morning."

If we ran late, we'd text profuse apologies—but we never ran late.

Then we'd pack our gear into Russ's orange Nissan Murano. He hated that car, one of Nissan's biggest-ever flops, but it had an AUX cable and heated seats, and I couldn't have been sorrier when Russ later sold it.

Before climbing in, we'd conduct an equipment double check, a custom arising from the time we went to Oneida Narrows on the Bear and I forgot my flyrod.

"Got your boots?"

"Yeah."

"Where's my vest? Here it is."

"VanZanten remembered his rod?"

"Go to hell. But yes."

I was permanently assigned to ride shotgun. Russ drove, and Brad sat in back. I periodically asked Brad if he wanted to trade, but he always said no. I'm a lot older than him, and although he was the better angler, he deferred to me as if the opposite were true.

(He doesn't anymore.)

In the car, we'd talk loudly and joke around. When you're fishing with buddies, irrational optimism builds like feedback between a guitar and amp. No matter what the signs, we'd interpret them as sure portents of a terrific day of fishing. As the river came into view, we transformed into highly skilled but entirely self-accredited entomologists, meteorologists and hydrologists.

"This cloud cover is gonna be perfect. Supposed to be in the seventies."

"Flows dropped. I checked the gage this morning."

"We'll definitely see some mayflies."

The river could be desiccated, filled in with concrete and on fire, and we'd still say, "Oh, yeah. This looks good."

The end came when Brad graduated—from college but also from the watershed. Russ put it best in an essay he wrote for the book we coauthored: "I knew Cache Valley couldn't keep Brad….He needed to find bigger water and bigger fish." Brad and Janelle moved to Montana, and Brad became a guide on the Missouri, which is another way of saying that they eventually got divorced.

Russ's patterns changed, too. When his daughter was born, his free time took a hard hit, and he fished less as she got older. Within a few years, my schedule rarely complemented Russ's, and as I recollect those days, I can't say when we last fished any local water together.

But we've never permanently disbanded. These days, we fish the Missouri River, and we fish annually instead of weekly—once per year, maybe twice. However, our outings have become decidedly grander, decidedly more like what Russ had in mind when he'd text us to say he'd wrangled a whole Saturday off.

The first time Russ and I visited Brad, we had to wait until September because we were all too busy to meet up in spring or summer. Brad drove us to various access points on the Missouri, mostly between Holter Dam and the little town of Craig, more like a fishing camp than a town, which consisted of three fly shops and two bars.

"I'm still trying to figure this place out," said Brad, but he put us on the fish.

From the high riverbanks we saw them—big, muscular trout feeding near the bottom in pods of four or five. Once we waded in, however, Russ and I were baffled by the long leaders Brad had built for us to nymph in the navel-deep lanes.

"There he is!" cried Brad as my indicator hesitated almost imperceptibly in the smooth, laminar flows.

"What?" I gasped.

Brad Hansen and Russ Beck on the Mo'.

"That was a fish. You missed him."

"That? That was a fish?"

"Yup. That fly is way far down. The indicator barely moves. You gotta really pay attention. There he is!"

"Wha?"

He laughed. "Another one."

When I began to actually detect these diffident takes, I'd play the big fish wrong, and they'd break off. I missed a dozen good fish that first morning. It didn't help that the autumn had given way already to winter, and any skills I might have used were eroded by the damp, hammering wind.

We scrambled up and down rip-rap banks and waded against the frigid press of the Missouri. Later in the day, Brad took us to the long flat run below Holter Dam, an imposing edifice that glowered in the distance beneath a ceiling of low clouds. I shuffled out into the dark water as far as my waders would take me, leaning steeply into the combined force of the current and unrelenting downriver wind. I felt as if the bumper of a truck was resting against my upstream hip and the driver was steadily pressing the gas pedal. We were swinging streamers, but I never dared turn my back to the dam, knowing that if I did, the current would blast the gravel from under my heels and I'd be launched boots-first into Craig. I got a solid bump on one of my final casts but was too demoralized to even mention it.

The second day it was warmer, and we kept several fish on our lines long enough to see them leap before they escaped. In the afternoon, the weather was calmer still, and we finally began landing trout.

Interlude beside the Missouri River.

As the sun came down into the open sky between the cloud cover and the crooked Montana horizon, I hooked a rainbow I estimated at twenty-two inches. I didn't land him, but I played him for several minutes, waiting as he peeled off yards of line against my drag and then reeling in when he hesitated. As he made what probably would've been his final dogged run, the fish jumped far clear of the water three times in rapid succession and shook my hook. Brad laughed and laughed before giving me a sympathetic slap on the back.

"You can count that one, Chadd," he said, still chuckling. "Long-distance release. You can count it."

I soon hooked another rainbow that I thought was even bigger. I played him the same way, and he, too, jumped cannily, but the hook stayed in. Brad was in position to net him. He turned out to be "only" about nineteen or twenty inches, but when I lifted the fish from the water, there was no give to him, like a flexed arm, no softness at all.

Soon we scaled the bank back up to Brad's car. After fishing for ten hours, I felt as if I'd been flogged.

In the years since then, our trips with Brad have often resulted in stories of blowing sleet and scarce fish. Brad says it's because we're always fishing in the shoulder seasons, the too-early spring, the too-late autumn, and the filthiest hot days of summer, when the fish are disgruntled and the resident anglers are all saying, "Shoulda been here last week."

But the shoulder seasons are all we can ever manage. Last year we tried like hell for a go in mid-June or late August, but we couldn't thread the

(*From bottom*): Chadd, Brad and Russ.

needle through the three separate schedules. We've transitioned into our own shoulder seasons—our families and jobs need us too much, and the weather and flow of our personal lives is never quite ideal.

When Russ and I finally got to Helena in 2019, it was October, but we got lucky that time. We encountered some sleet, but on the first day, we also brought around fifty Missouri River browns and rainbows to Brad's driftboat, and on day two, Brad took us back to Holter Dam, where we each caught five or six fish apiece, all of which were eighteen to twenty inches.

"Pretty sure that's the best fishing I've seen up here in a while," said Brad. "Not bad for shoulder season."

Whether floating the Mo' or wading the freestone creeks of the Bear River watershed, all of our trips end the same way. The insoluble catch-22 of fishing: when the fishing is good, you stay out longer, but when it's bad, you stay out longer. So, we stay out longer, waiting almost until dark to head back.

In the failing light, we're slower to break down our gear than we were setting it up. We're quieter, too. Russ finds a crumpled sack of chips and shakes the last powdery shards into his mouth. I tilt back my seat to sleep but then stay awake and talk, yawning mid-sentence and running a hand over my face. We find a restaurant and order steaks and beer, and we're drowsing before the food arrives.

If the fishing was good, we retell the tales, entering them into the team's shared memory.

"That one by the bridge. He was just waiting. Slammed it."

"What fly'd he take?"

"That big wire worm. Just slammed it. I felt it in my shoulder."

If the fishing was poor, we console ourselves.

"We caught a couple, at least."

"Sure, couple nice ones."

I don't know if we'll ever get together in June. We seem consigned to our places among the shoulder seasons. After another trip or two, I might even take a liking to the icy currents, obstinate fish and scooping sleet from my eye sockets.

As we collect our gear to part ways, we say, "Great trip, though. God, yeah. Let's go again. Yeah, soon."

And then we head home, where we wait for Russ to text again.

3.

ADMONITION FOR
THE ANTHROPOCENE AGE

’ve always had a fondness for Black Friday.

Yes, I’m talking about opening day of the American yuletide retail orgy, when U.S. shoppers slip out into the raw predawn blackness to line up in the nation’s big-box parking lots and, mere hours after Thanksgiving, prepare to batter each other aside for their share of the season’s niftiest consumer goods. There is something muscular about shopping-related casualties, something essentially American about Black Friday.

And every year, I make sure I’m nowhere near any of it.

In fact, I refer to Black Friday as "Brown Friday," because it’s a day I set aside to go fishing for spawning brown trout on the Logan River in northern Utah. (If you’re raising your hand to object to targeting spawning fish, I’ll be with you in a moment.)

My buddy Donicio Gomez turned me on to the Logan River brown trout spawn. This was years ago. Back then, he worked at the local fly shop and was a native of Colorado, so it seems appropriate that he’d show me how to fish for nonnatives. Donicio himself looked like a nonnative in his silky sports jerseys, basketball shorts and designer flip-flops, which he often wore even while fishing. The first time I saw him at the flyshop, I figured he must be a member of some Long Beach surf shop salesclerk exchange program. His eyeglasses had thick black frames, the kind the guy in RUN-DMC used to wear, and he always wore a ballcap with a flat brim.

On the back of a sales receipt, he sketched the Logan River spawn-fishing rig he’d perfected.

Logan River brown trout.

"Okay, so, this is just like you know an old leader that's been cut down to four feet and maybe like 2X," Donicio began, drawing a long line. "Tie some 3X below that, like three feet." He drew a small circle—"Indicator. Adjust to depth."

His precise pen strokes suggested that he'd drawn this diagram a few times before.

"Put your splitshot like one dollar bill up from the fly," he said, scribbling a black dot. (Donicio used money and currency-related items as units of measurement.)

"Put a couple splitshots above that." He scribbled two more dots. "Like about one credit card apart."

Next came a size-14 Glo Bug (the egg pattern popularized and stigmatized by Howell Raines), preferably tied somewhat carelessly in a hard-to-find shade of neon pink peach yarn.

"You can drop an olive Woolly Bugger off the egg," Donicio added, sketching. "Unweighted. Up to you."

Appropriately, the rig was called the Christmas Tree.

"Cast it with the good ole chuck-and-duck," Donicio advised, simulating how to trail the tackle downstream to load the rod and then heave the complicated rig festively upstream. The Woolly Bugger imitated a nest-raiding sculpin in hot pursuit a mere three dollar-bill widths behind the fugitive yarn egg—a tiny, aquatic Christmastime chase scene with every cast.

I fished the brown trout spawn on the Logan River for many seasons. And if you've still got your hand in the air about spawn-fishing, just hang on. Because it was more than just a way to cushion the miserable onset of Christmas at the expense of lots of sex-crazed brown trout. There was something about Logan Canyon that was coldly welcoming in November—like the cordially indifferent, locals-only welcome you get at the drafty neighborhood dive bar.

The Logan River rises in Idaho at an elevation of 8,096 feet and runs almost immediately into Utah, where it flows fifty-four miles down through the wide valleys and almost indecent scenic immensity of Logan Canyon in the Bear River Mountains, which feature soaring limestone and dolomite formations and forests of pine, spruce, juniper and aspen. Visitors come from great distances to take in the canyon's fall colors, and that section of U.S. Highway 89 is a National Scenic Byway.

The river was first called the Little Bear River but was later named for Ephraim Logan, one of the first mountain men to trap beaver in Cache Valley in the 1820s. The overwhelming majority of the river flows within the public lands of Wasatch-Cache National Forest. Angler access is ubiquitous until the river exits the canyon and enters the city of Logan, where access is downgraded to merely abundant.

Although it's one of the largest rivers in the Bear River watershed, the Logan is not a tributary of the Bear itself—the Logan is intercepted five

Logan Canyon, circa 1900. *Courtesy of USU Special Collections, Merrill-Cazier Library.*

miles west of Logan by the river *now* known as the Little Bear River, which then flows into the marshy flats of Cache Valley before mingling with the Bear River.

At the end of October, when I'd be gearing up for the browns, the Logan was near base flow, the water clear and the autumn foliage transitioning from signature scarlets and golds to shades of brown and tan. The fair-weather anglers would've been gone since Labor Day, and after the snows arrived, most of the hardcore locals would hang it up, too. The river was practically vacant as the brown trout staged up, and when they began to spawn, the Christmas Tree put fifty-fish days within reach in river sections where twenty-fish days were often rare.

By late November, winter storms lumbered through with some regularity. The sky was often overcast on those mornings, and the light was flat and omnidirectional, causing the neon-colored yarn eggs to fluoresce. From fifty feet off, I could watch the egg splash down, sink through the clear water and then bounce lightly over the gravelly spawning beds like a pink Pachinko ball. Big spawners would traverse a fifty-foot channel to scoop it up.

Temperatures during the spawn were frequently below freezing, which meant ice in the rod guides. If it dropped below about twenty degrees, ice encased the flyline, too. There might be hazardous ice at the banks, and there might be a storm howling directly downcanyon for my own individual enjoyment. It was at least predictable: I could predict with certainty that I'd catch lots of fish and freeze my ass off. I came to think of late autumn as the canyon's default mood—cold, earth-tone mornings dusted with white, the mountains dark and damp-looking, stark against brooding skies.

As to those objections. Many anglers disapprove of fishing for spawning trout, which is to say, they'd sooner sleep with their sister than cast to redds. I get it. Spawning trout are nearly defenseless, out of their minds with sexual urges and fishing for them can feel like a dirty trick. Some view it as unethical. Others say it's simply uncouth, a half-step above fishing with treble hooks and PowerBait. I really do get it.

But in defense of fishing for spawning browns, I would raise a few points. First, many other fish species are targeted during their spawning seasons. Every steelhead taken from fresh water is taken from a spawning run. Salmon migrations are, obviously, spawning events. And, personally, I don't think you've had any real fun until you've cast a foam popper at big spring bluegills bedding testily on redds. In fresh water and at sea, recreationally and commercially, targeting spawning fish might be the most common strategy in all the universe of fishing.

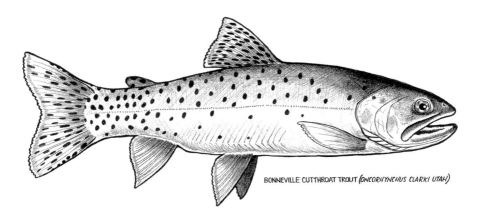

BONNEVILLE CUTTHROAT TROUT *(ONCORHYNCHUS CLARKI UTAH)*

If the "everyone else does it" defense doesn't do it for you, I'll point out that fishing the brown trout spawn in the Logan River is permitted and even gently encouraged by the Division of Wildlife, which furnishes information about the spawn's timing, locations and fishing tips.

But the final argument rises to the level of conservational imperative, which is that in the Logan River and throughout the Bear River watershed, nonnative brown trout currently threaten the persistence of the indigenous trout species: the Bear River Bonneville cutthroat.

This is no new allegation. They've been at this for more than a century. Brown trout were introduced to the United States by way of Michigan in 1883, and by 1900, they were in thirty-eight states plus Puerto Rico. Today, browns have been found in almost all fifty states, including Hawaii. Only Alaska, Louisiana and Mississippi are as yet considered brown trout free.

Browns have driven native fish species to extirpation throughout the western United States, but it can be argued that in most of their range, they are no longer really invading. The great Eurasian brown trout invasion is pretty much over, and the browns won. The subsequent loss of native species is part of our settled conservational past.

Comprehensive eradication of brown trout from the United States was probably never an ecologically practical option, and there'd be insufficient public support to try it today, even if it were. In Montana and Wyoming, for example, brown trout have been treated like beloved de facto natives for a very long time. Fly-fishing writer Ted Leeson says he prefers catching brown trout to all other salmonids, including the native cutthroat, steelhead and salmon of his own northwestern homewaters.

It's a little different on the Logan River. Brown trout arrived in the Bear River watershed in the late 1890s or early 1900s, but they are, technically, still invading. Brown trout can be caught in every corner of the watershed—from the tiniest tributaries to the deepest, muddiest sections of the mainstem Bear. The Bonneville cutthroat trout population of the Logan River is still holding out against the browns and has been for something like 120 years.

The native cutthroats are entrenched in the higher, colder reaches of the Logan. The brown trout are firmly established in the lower river, where the water is warmer, deeper and dirtier. Every year, however, the browns push a little higher up the river. Presently, the invasion front lies about fourteen miles up Logan Canyon, about halfway to the summit, at an area called Twin Bridges. Here they clash over a sort of no-trout's-land.

I spoke about this to Dr. Phaedra Budy, the leading fish ecology researcher at Utah State University. Tall, with straight blond hair, Budy is an outdoorsy, hands-on scientist who resembles nothing so much as a seasoned Nordic alpinist. She confirmed that the browns have pressed their invasion halfway up Logan Canyon, but she was quick to refine that characterization.

"The interface *is* at Twin Bridges," Budy confirmed, "but it's not distinct anymore. There are more brown trout higher up in the river, but there aren't more cutthroats lower down. It's very much an asymmetrical interface."

With her hands, Budy pantomimed a set of scales skewed to one side.

"In other words," she said, "cutthroats are bothered by browns, but the browns are not bothered by cutthroats."

That's because the brown trout are tougher and meaner than cutthroats. Browns tolerate lower water quality and wider swings in water temperature. Most significantly, browns are aggressive—they attack the docile cutts, not just by preying on them but also by driving them from the favorable habitat all trout need to feed and rest.

In a 2016 study at Utah State University, rather mouthfully titled "Can High Densities of Native Trout Minimize Negative Impacts of Exotic Trout Through Biotic Resistance?," fish researcher W. Carl Saunders used large cattle-watering tanks as artificial habitats to observe small populations of trout arranged into various ratios of cutthroats and browns. In each tank, Saunders placed three, four, five or six cutthroats. To each of these groups, he added two brown trout. And then he watched.

Saunders found that cutthroats were best able to resist brown trout harassment when they outnumbered the browns by two-to-one or more. At the less-favorable ratio (three-to-two), the cutthroats suffered significantly from brown trout attacks, which Saunders measured in terms of health metrics like fish weight, growth and mortality. And even when the browns were outnumbered three-to-one, the cutts never seemed to bother the browns.

Simply put, only at high densities can cutthroats mount an effective resistance against nonnatives, but even then, they don't retaliate—the hardship is simply shared by more individual cutthroats. Unfortunately, native cutthroats tend to naturally settle into low-density populations, so they'll likely always be easy targets for brown trout invasion.

But the cutts aren't helpless. They might not be clutch fighters in one-on-one brawls with browns, but cutthroats do exist at relatively high densities in the upper Logan. They're also resilient as a species, having already survived many egregious environmental insults before brown trout were ever released in Michigan.

"From 1860 to 1910, Mormon settlers overused or misused the Bear River Range's lumber, grazing forage, wild game, and water resources and introduced invasive plant and animal species throughout the area." That's from "An Environmental History of the Bear River Range, 1860–1910," the master's thesis of historian and Missouri River fly-fishing guide Brad Hansen. Brad's a fishing buddy of mine, and in his writing, I detect what I'd call bemused discontent as he recounts a remorseless encroachment on the Bear River watershed, not by brown trout but by Mormons—timber clear-cutting, wholesale logging, overfishing, overgrazing, overhunting and pell-mell constructing dams. The Mormon settlers brutalized the Bear River Bonneville cutthroat trout, and somehow, they're still here.

The upside is what Budy calls a "conservational movement to shift angler focus back to native trout." A century after we humans brought in brown trout to lay siege to Logan River, we've switched sides, and now we back the cutthroats.

Budy herself is probably the most diligent ally the cutthroats could hope for. In fact, she and her partners (including local anglers) are responsible for the single-most successful native cutthroat recovery effort in the Bear River watershed: the Right Fork Project.

It began in 2003 with data collection and monitoring. In 2009, volunteers and agency personnel began removing brown trout from Right Fork, a small tributary of the Logan River in the "brown trout zone," downstream from the invasion interface. Around the same time, fertile cutthroats were taken from the upper Logan, and their eggs were collected, fertilized, incubated and hatched. In 2012, a barrier was constructed at the downstream end of Right Fork to stop brown trout from reinvading it from the Logan River. Finally, in 2013, all fish were removed from Right Fork and then replaced with the 2,500 to 4,000 cutthroat eggs and fry from the previously mentioned egg collections.

Electrofishing efforts during the Right Fork Project.

This not only restored Right Fork to a more natural, locals-only condition, but it also transformed the small tributary into a native trout nursery; mature native cutts can move down into the Logan River to join the resistance behind enemy lines, but the barrier prevents brown trout from ever reappropriating Right Fork.

Budy said that by 2018 Right Fork's native cutthroat population had grown to half the stream's carrying capacity and could be near its full capacity by around 2030. She was too scientifically reticent to make specific forecasts regarding if or how the project might redraw the battle lines in the war against brown trout, but she's not just waiting around for monitoring results either. Instead, she's presenting the Right Fork Project as an example of how truly resilient native freshwater fish worldwide can be. It's an admonition for the Anthropocene Age, the present geologic period characterized by large-scale, human-made environmental change.

"The Logan River is pretty special," said Budy. "It has pristine habitat, holds lots of snowpack and has strong spring inputs that keep the water cold and relatively productive, which will be important as temperatures [globally] continue to rise. The Logan could become a sanctuary for Bonneville cutthroat."

Nor is Budy finished with the Logan River. Her newest project calls for mechanical removal and selective exclusion of brown trout from Temple Fork, another Logan River tributary and the most important spawning area for native cutts. After the browns have been removed, a selective fish gate would be installed, which would allow only cutthroats to pass upstream, and another tributary (this one upstream of the interface, in the cutthroat zone) would be returned to a more natural, pre-brown-trout condition.

Budy's vision extends to the Bear River watershed too. "There are no fluvial cutthroats in the Logan River anymore," she said, referring to the large-bodied, big-river variety of Bonneville cutthroats that once roamed widely throughout the Bear River, swimming miles to and from high-elevation tributaries to spawn. Budy explained that the dams and other developments have spoiled the hydraulic connections that allowed fluvial Bonneville cutthroats long ago to come and go freely from the Bear to the Logan and other tributaries.

"But," she added, "fluvial cutthroats could come back really quickly if those connections were reestablished. It seems to be something they're hardwired for. As soon as they're given another chance at it, they're ready."

It's difficult to say what that chance would look like. It'd require dam removal, river restoration and extensive additional cutthroat recovery. It would be costly and time consuming, and it would happen at the expense of a lot more Logan River brown trout than I've ever annoyed by fishing in their spawning grounds on Brown Friday.

Logan River fly anglers don't despise brown trout, but the Logan is certainly not a brown trout river. If an angler on the Logan River is visiting

Bear River Bonneville cutthroat trout. *Courtesy of Klaus VanZanten.*

from more than two hours away, it's to catch genetically pure Bear River Bonneville cutthroat trout. Local anglers likewise treat the cutthroats with conservational reverence. We seldom harvest them, for instance, even though it's legal to do so. We instead call them "Bonnies" and show them extreme courtesy, like gentlemen callers fawning over the town belle, throwing topcoats onto mudpuddles and scurrying ahead to open doors for her.

Still, claiming that I fish the Logan River brown spawn because I want to help native trout would be like pretending I eat steak because I'm crazy about the National Cattlemen's Beef Association. I fish the spawn because it's fun. But the cutthroats can indeed use any advantage they can get, so maybe that's why I'm not paralyzed with guilt when I hook a two-pound spawning brown on a yarn egg from a stretch of river that should be full of two-pound cutties. Call it my Christmas card to the Bonneville cutthroat trout. Budy's right—the focus really has shifted to the native species. As anglers in these parts cast to spawning browns, we think about what it'd be like to restore those hydraulic connections and give the Bear River back to the fluvial cutthroats. I used to think it couldn't happen in my lifetime, but after listening to Phaedra Budy, I'm not so sure.

"These native fish populations have suffered so many ecological consequences," she said. "We tend to think that they're really delicate, but they're not. They're highly resilient. You take away the impacts or restore the habitat, and they bounce right back."

That is something I'd get up early for and stand in a long cold line to see.

4.

A CERTAIN DESOLATION

My earliest recollection of Bear Lake is camping there when I was eleven years old the summer after my family moved to Utah from Oakland, California. We had a green Chevy pickup with a camper on the back. My parents let me and my older brother, Richard, ride back there, which I'm sure was illegal, even in the 1980s. The sleeping compartment over the cab had forward-facing louvered windows. We cranked them wide open and stuck our faces into the blast like dogs on a car ride.

A more recent Bear Lake memory is from January a few years ago. My friend Andrew invited me to fish the lake one bitter Sunday morning.

"The sculpin are spawning," he'd told me, "on the east side where it drops off into the deep part. The big cutthroats come up to that edge to hunt. You throw a streamer out there, and dude, it's on."

He explained that this deep-winter technique was one of the few ways to fly-fish for Bear Lake's adfluvial (lake-dwelling) Bonneville cutthroat trout. We met at 6:00 a.m. in Logan Canyon and drove over the mountain in Andrew's truck.

Bear Lake is eighteen miles long and seven miles wide, a north-south oblong straddling the Utah-Idaho border along the eastern foot of the Bear River Mountains. The Bear Lake overlook, where U.S. Highway 89 comes out of Logan Canyon, is two thousand feet higher than the valley below and offers a comprehensive view of the one-hundred-square-mile lake.

As our camper surmounted the overlook, we saw the lake shining in the sun like a gemstone the size of a city. Dad drove down around the lake's southern lobe to a campground on the east bank. Richard and I tried fishing with our spinning gear, but we'd been taught to cast at weed beds and tree stumps. Bear Lake offered only a monotonous and featureless strand of jagged rocks like shattered bricks. We didn't catch anything.

Richard grabbed a six-pack of Mello Yello from the cooler and we got into our two-person rubber raft with our spinning rods and rowed up the beach. The water was so clear that we could see the bottom twenty-five feet down.

Andrew said, "Lake's looking good this year."

Visitors to Bear Lake often gasp audibly at their first sight of the lake's blue color (the result of sunlight refracting in the limestone-rich water), but that's not what Andrew was doing. The lake was leaden that morning, reflecting the overcast sky. He was instead observing a local custom, which is to remark on Bear Lake's water level upon seeing it from the overlook. During the past twenty years, the lake level has fluctuated shockingly because of droughts. With just a glance, locals can assess whether the lake is "looking good" or "looking low" or somewhere in between.

I nodded at Andrew's appraisal. The lake looked much better than ten years ago, when piers and docks lay in the sand among willow saplings a quarter-mile from the water's edge. Back then people at least seemed concerned about Bear Lake's health. Now that it was filling up, it'd attracted attention of another kind. In 2018, the Utah Division of Water Resources and Idaho Water Resources Board filed an application with the Utah Division of Water Rights to appropriate four hundred thousand acre-feet of "unclaimed" Bear Lake water.

A hot wind blew from the southeast, not strong enough to raise much chop but enough to push our raft away from the rocky shore, first fifty yards and then one hundred. We couldn't see the bottom anymore. Beneath us was only an empty blue expanse, an inverted sky.

We'd heard Bear Lake had its own monster, like Loch Ness, and we'd both seen *Jaws*, but while I recall the vertigo of open water, I don't remember feeling afraid. Richard and I were strong swimmers; we swam in the ocean back in California. Mostly, I suspect, we relied on the bluffed-up courage of brothers—each stifling our fear for the benefit of the other. We fished some more but still caught nothing.

To understand how four hundred thousand acre-feet of water can be unclaimed, an explanation of the relationship between the Bear River, Bear Lake and Great Salt Lake might be useful.

At 250,000 years of age, Bear Lake is one of North America's oldest lakes. It once connected to the Bear River, but 11,000 years ago, sediment deposits separated the two, and separate they remained until the late 1880s, when agricultural developers saw the potential of storing Bear River water in Bear Lake. The two were only nine miles apart. So, in the late 1890s, Bear Lake was dammed, and it rose ten feet. Then, in 1911, Stewart Dam was built on the Bear River, with inlet and outlet canals, which to this day, divert the entire river into the lake and then back out. (The river between the canals is dewatered.) Thus the Bear River, Bear Lake and Great Salt Lake were joined in a gigantic Faustian railroad, delivering irrigation water and hydroelectricity to the entire region.

The system is currently operated by energy giant PacifiCorp, but it's been regulated since 1958 by the Bear River Compact, a multistate agreement that divvies up the Bear River watershed drop by drop.

According to the compact, Bear Lake is said to be full at 5,923.65 feet of elevation. However, PacifiCorp doesn't allow it to rise that high to avoid the risk of spring flooding downstream, for which PacifiCorp might be held liable. So, PacifiCorp set a target elevation of 5,918 feet. When the water rises above that, the excess is released into the Bear River. The difference between the full and target elevations is 5.65 feet, which equates to the aforementioned 400,000 acre-feet of water.

However, that water is largely hypothetical. The lake doesn't hit the target elevation every year and hasn't been full since the mid-1980s.

Here's the rub: any excess water that *does* manage to accumulate is customarily released during winter, when downstream users don't need water and have nowhere to store it, so it flows through the system and to Great Salt Lake. Hence, in the opinion of Utah and Idaho's water agencies, any of that four hundred thousand acre-feet that makes it to Great Salt Lake is "going to waste"—and they want it.

We languished in the raft like castaways. We'd been gone for hours. Stately sailboats glided by us. The sun blazed down. We swam around our raft and drank Mello Yello to cool off. Speedboats seethed across the water, and the raft rocked on their wakes.

"We're pretty far," I said. "We should go back."

Richard agreed. We paddled furiously for shore, but our arms went rubbery before we made any appreciable progress, and the wind took over again. We trailed our arms in the water and gazed over the side at the featureless floor of sand.

"Hey," I said, "I see the bottom."

We'd drifted into shallower water. The shadow of the raft glided across the lakebed like that of a zeppelin.

Richard pointed and said, "Look. What's down there?"

I looked. Dozens of little round things scattered across the bottom, pure white, the size of tennis balls or maybe chicken eggs.

"They look like eggs," I said.

"No," Richard scoffed. "How could they be eggs?"

In one sense, these four hundred thousand acre-feet of water are already claimed by the Bear River and Great Salt Lake. It's corny to say the water belongs to nature, but *any* water that makes it through the gauntlet of Bear River diversions and dams to Great Salt Lake is a boon to both waterways, which support a panoply of life—native fish, ten million migratory birds and an immense complex of wetlands.

Why did Utah and Idaho lay claim to the water? It's difficult to say, because they state no justifications. In their application, the spaces provided to explain the "Purpose and Extent of Use" were left blank. No purpose, no plan. Additional text in an attachment manages to provide even less information, stating cryptically that the water will be used for "existing and future water uses" and stored for "Municipal Storage." In other words, the water will be used for uses and stored for storage.

At the rec center in Oakland, both Richard and I could dive to the bottom of the deep end of the swimming pool. We'd throw our Hot Wheels in and dive twelve feet down to retrieve them. The lake didn't seem much deeper, so we dove in. First Richard and then me. We gulped air, dove off the raft and then kicked like hell, arms flat to our sides.

But we couldn't reach the bottom. We'd get within three feet and then have to turn around and claw for the surface. We emerged gasping.

"They gotta be eggs," I panted, resurfacing after a close attempt.

"How could they be?" Richard repeated. "Buncha eggs sitting in a lake? No way."

We drifted farther, and the lakebed rose imperceptibly beneath us.

"Wait a second," said Richard peering into the water. "I know what they are."

The raft made a poor diving platform. It was wobbly and it half submerged every time we pushed off. Several inches of water sloshed around inside.

But Richard made a clean dive and scuba-kicked straight down. I watched from the raft, wanting him to make it and not wanting him to. He made it. A cloud of sediment bloomed beneath him as he plucked an egg from the bottom. Then he flip turned and launched upward, bubbles trailing from his nose. He broke the surface spluttering, hair slick over his face and clutching the prize triumphantly in his fist.

"Golf balls!" he hollered, streaming water as he hauled himself into the raft.

The ball was white and imprinted with red stripes and a little golden crown. I immediately plunged in, kicking madly. As I descended, water pressure squeezed my eardrums and sinuses. I focused on a single blurry white blob, but the deeper I dove, the slower I swam. My lungs were depleted. At last, I reached the bottom. The raft hovered high above me. Grab, flip turn, launch.

Utah water rights attorney Emily Lewis explained the unclaimed water this way: "They're trying to 'make' more water by increasing storage capacity in Bear Lake. When they say they'll 'use it for uses,' they're not trying to be cute—'beneficial use' means consumptive, primarily commercial ways to use water. If in-stream flow was a beneficial use in Utah, any or all of that water could be sent to the Great Salt Lake."

Not everyone is so sanguine. Friends of Great Salt Lake, a nonprofit conservation group, has filed a protest against the application. In a 2018 newspaper article, Friends director Lynn de Freitas said, "I don't know exactly what it all means. I don't even know if the Division of Water Resources knows what it means."

Did the Utah Division of Water Resources file its application simply because it was being "wasted" on Great Salt Lake? Or for nobler reasons? Such a water reserve would benefit farmers during droughts, but that's precisely when the Bear River and Great Salt Lake ecosystems need water too.

This might look different if Utah and Idaho were doing everything possible to conserve water. If they were metering all irrigation and growing water-wise crops but still needed more water, this claim would make more sense. But that's not the case. Utah and Idaho are, respectively, the second and ninth most arid of the states, yet their per capita water usage ranks second and first, respectively. Farmers in the region grow many crops that are utterly ill suited for the arid West, including alfalfa, which requires nearly as much water as rice.

But to tackle water scarcity in Utah, Lewis said, you can't work outside western water law. "Prior appropriation doctrine is the law of the land,"

East bank of Bear Lake.

she said, referring to the foundational, first-come, first-serve principle of western water law. "If you want in-stream flows, you have to work within the system by acquiring water rights, then establishing in-stream flow as a beneficial use."

Easier said than done, said de Freitas. "To try to change the Compact, to make water for Great Salt Lake a beneficial use—you might as well fly to Mars. Let's not be blind. Great Salt Lake has dropped eleven feet since [the arrival of White settlers]. We're in serious decline. We have to find and maintain a range of elevations, a sweet spot, where the lake can do what it needs to do as an ecosystem and a natural resource."

This is also easier said than done, said Lewis: "People don't understand the scale of that problem. To raise the Great Salt Lake by just one foot, you need 120,000 acre-feet of *depletion*, not just diversion. That would effectively take 64,000 acres of agriculture—alfalfa, mint, onions—out of production, a majority of the total agriculture of the watershed. You would need widespread, unprecedented cooperation."

The raft drifted from the east bank on the Utah side, across the state line into Idaho, over the lake's open water and greatest depths and on north to the vast flats of North Beach, a distance of ten miles. We'd put ourselves in terrible danger—there are drowning accidents on Bear Lake almost every year involving people wearing life jackets in seaworthy watercraft that nevertheless capsize in rough water driven by the lake's notorious winds. Richard and I were more concerned with how much trouble we were in (which, it turned out, was considerable). But now we spotted people and boats on North Beach a few hundred yards away.

So, we worked like divers over an oyster bed, retrieving the absurd, plastic-skinned pearls. The water was so shallow we no longer needed the raft to dive. With a few kicks, we shot to the lakebed with enough air to collect two or three balls at once. They knocked around in the flooded bottom of the raft like an insane aquatic version of billiards.

I don't know why we thought it was such an opulent discovery. We'd seen kids selling buckets of golf balls on roadsides near golf courses; perhaps we thought we'd sell the trove, make a whole five bucks each. I suspect it had more to do with the childish view that the golf balls were simply there, up for grabs.

Andrew pulled off the road at Cisco Beach. It was the same monotonous beach of brick fragments Richard and I had fished long ago. I'd been to Bear Lake many times since but mostly to North Beach, seldom to the east bank. I gazed in the direction the little raft had drifted. The damp easterly wind howled, and the cold rocks clanked beneath our wading boots as we walked to the shoreline. We waded thirty feet into the water and cast long for the drop-off, which was a vague band of indigo one hundred feet out. Andrew's double-haul was superb. His clean, quick form shot half again as much line as mine. Cold crept in through my waders and thermals.

Andrew gave me a fly he'd tied called the Balanced Minnow. The hook was angled and weighted to orient horizontally in the water to more closely resemble one of Bear Lake's four endemic fish species: Bear Lake sculpin, Bear Lake whitefish, Bonneville whitefish and Bonneville cisco. They use the rock beaches for spawning. The small, herring-like cisco famously appears by late January, washing up onto its namesake beach. It's permissible to capture up to thirty of them using a dip net. Locals call it the Cisco Disco.

There is no endemic species of cutthroat in Bear Lake, but it does contain the Bear Lake strain of Bonneville cutthroat, the adfluvial fish Andrew and I had come to catch.

And of which we caught none.

We worked at it for a couple hours, though. The wind was at our backs, a kindness to my subpar distance casting, but it also lent the trip a certain desolation.

Bear Lake.

Andrew had warned me. "Even if the fish're active," he'd said, "we might only land one or two." I took comfort in this—regardless of fish caught or missed, the misery would at least be over before lunch.

"Once it starts getting light," explained Andrew, "the big fish drop back down. If they're really hitting, we might go 'til eleven, but we'll probably be back in town by then."

I was ready to leave at nine but kept casting, waiting for Andrew to call it.

"I think I felt a bump," he said.

"Yeah? A fish?"

"Maybe. Could be. Guess it's a little slow."

To stay warm, I thought of that blistering day when my father located Richard and me sunburnt and drowsy at North Beach after being lost at sea all afternoon.

Andrew reeled in his line. "We must'a hit it a little too late, dude," he said apologetically. "The timing's off this year. It's been weird."

I hear that a lot lately. Practically every angler I know has a story of a fishery that has declined in the past decade. The fish, water and weather don't behave like they used to.

"It's been weird."

Andrew moved to Nevada, leaving me to prospect for Bear Lake's adfluvial cutts on my own the following December. I did all right. Andrew said we might hook only one or two fish per morning. I fished twice that next winter and caught one impressive adfluvial cutthroat each day. I haven't decided for sure whether that trip is worth it.

Along with the endemic fishes, there are native and endemic crustaceans in Bear Lake, small ones, several of which are said to have been extinct or extirpated sometime in the early 1900s, soon after the Bear River was diverted into the lake. That's all it took. Delicate aquatic species are much more sensitive to minor variations in water quality and temperature than, say, the seemingly indestructible whitefish. But Bear Lake's tiny aquatic fauna were only the very first casualties of this weird new era, marked not by super-slow geology but by eye-blink Anthropocene transformations.

With the ability to artificially connect one colossal ecosystem to another for no better reason than to grow sugar beets, such monumental and irreversible consequences should come as no surprise. With the prerogative to claim and displace half a million acre-feet of water as though it were some stray freight car in a railyard, compounded by the stressors of resource scarcity and climate change, who can say which waterway or ecosystem will be up for grabs next, or which species will be next to vanish?

Adfluvial Bear Lake Bonneville cutthroat trout. *Courtesy of Kyle Jensen.*

5.

MASSACRE AT BOA OGOI

Whenever I cross over the Utah-Idaho border, I see Shoshone warriors. Astride bareback ponies, they watch from the bluffs overlooking U.S. Highway 89 as I drive north into Franklin. I see Shoshone women harvesting wild grain from the sea of grass beneath Little Mountain. Hunting parties patrol the riverbanks along the streams where I fish. Larger groups depart eastward to hunt bison in Wyoming.

And I see bears. Grizzlies stalk the brushy mazes of Willow Flat. Sows lead their bumbling cubs up Logan Canyon to feast on spawning Bonneville cutthroat.

The Shoshone aren't really there, of course, and neither are the bears. But whenever I go into the wilds, my imagination divests the land of civilization. I squint to see it as it was before.

I'm no anthropologist or wildlife biologist, so my imaginings might be highly inaccurate. However, the Shoshone called the Bear River *Boa Ogoi*, meaning "Big River," and French-Canadian fur trapper Michael Bourdon named it the Bear River for its bear population, so I don't think any credentials are needed to picture indigenous people living in Cache Valley along the large and fertile river, surrounded by a thriving bear population.

But the bears and Shoshone were driven off long ago—the former by pioneers, the latter by the U.S. Army.

Predators were removed from Cache Valley to make it safer for livestock, but according to historian Brad Hansen, it began in the winter of 1863 as a gory competition between the valley's southern and northern residents.

Hundreds of men on horseback swept at close ranks through Cache Valley, merrily blasting and bludgeoning coyotes, wolves, bears, mountain lions and even lynx. Hansen states these were likely "ring hunts," in which horsemen encircled a wide area and then advanced on their quarry in an ever-diminishing ring. The team committing the most mayhem was honored with a victory dinner and dance. This pioneer Super Bowl of death was observed until the turn of the century.

The struggle between early settlers and nature is most sensationalized in the legend of Old Ephraim, an enormous grizzly, the last of his kind reported in Cache Valley. Said to stand ten feet tall and weigh half a ton, this mythic creature plundered livestock and menaced settlers from Soda Springs to Ogden. Supposedly endowed with malevolent and preternatural intelligence, Old Ephraim evaded traps and hunters for decades, until he was brought down in 1923 after a heroic fracas with lowly sheep rancher Frank Clark, who was armed with only a varmint rifle and a hunting dog. In 1966, a monument to Old Ephraim's memory was erected in Logan Canyon, and part of the bear's skull is on exhibit in a library at Utah State University.

Today, Cache Valley remains virtually free of apex predators.

Considering it was Europeans who named the Bear River, the eradication of its bear population by its European population is not without irony. It might even engender resentment toward early settlers, particularly Mormons, because although all immigrants to the American West worked hard to tame it, to press it into productivity, the religious immigrant is especially rapacious, seizing land by claiming a god told him to. Mormon settlers believed they'd be promoted to gods themselves in the hereafter, with the ability to create their own planets. Earthly life was for them a mere probation during which sixty years of concerted industry earned them an eternity of galactic wealth and power. Thus afterlife-leaning Mormon homesteaders didn't trouble themselves over the earthly consequences of shooting a bear. And after they'd extinguished the predators, they went to work on the fish population, damming streams and introducing a fellow European colonizer, the brown trout, which would not so much exterminate the native Bonneville cutthroat trout as supplant it and out compete it.

But the loss of wildlife and introduction of nonnative species, while regrettable, is of little importance when compared to the Bear River Massacre, now thought of as the deadliest attack on indigenous people in American history. It occurred in 1863, the same year the Bear River predator eradications began, and for the same purpose—to rid the region of "undesirables."

The most complete account of the tragedy is Brigham D. Madsen's *The Shoshoni Frontier and the Bear River Massacre*. Published in 1985 and meticulously documented, Madsen's book tells how a detachment from the California Volunteers of the U.S. Army, disgruntled at being passed over for more illustrious assignments in the Civil War, obtained official clearance to destroy the first band of natives they could build a case against.

Madsen indicts the Mormon settlers for their part in the massacre. When Mormons moved into Cache Valley in the early 1850s, it was the lush and sacred mountain refuge of the Northwestern Shoshone. Mormon prophet Brigham Young preached that it was less expensive to feed the Natives than fight them, so at first, Cache Valley enjoyed relative peace. Mormons maintained their divine right to appropriate Shoshone land without asking or paying for it, but they at least assisted the Shoshone they displaced by periodically distributing food, clothing and other necessaries. This didn't last. As the struggling Shoshone begged for more aid to fend off destitution, even Young viewed Mormon charity as a "severe tax" and condoned greater use of force.

By 1861, Cache Valley's game was vanishing. The grassland, a critical source of forage for the Shoshone themselves, was infested with insatiable livestock. The settlers were not so much exterminating the Shoshone as supplanting them, out competing them. Madsen states that "a spirit of violent solutions" soon prevailed, and the desperate Shoshone people increasingly resorted to larceny and violence, which led to deadly cycles of misdirected retaliation.

In January 1863, members of the Northwestern Shoshone band were implicated in a series of bloody raids. This was the outrage the California Volunteers had been waiting to avenge, and so at 6:00 a.m. on January 29, they initiated a frontal assault on an encampment at the confluence of the Bear River and Battle Creek near Preston, Idaho, where about 450 Northwestern Shoshone were lodged for winter. Shoshone leader Sagwitch Timbimboo, an early riser, spotted the smoking breath of cavalry riders and horses. He raised an alarm. The Shoshone, fielding approximately 200 warriors, mounted a passable early defense, firing from the cover of the banks of Battle Creek. However, with superior weaponry and war fighting ability, the U.S. force flanked the Shoshone and dismantled their defenses with enfilading fire. As the volunteers pressed the advantage, Madsen argues, the attack became a massacre, and the massacre became a slaughter.

It's true that indigenous people of North America and European settlers had already been treating each other with unspeakable brutality for centuries. Rape, torture and murder were so commonplace that they were practically forms of currency. However, Mormonism again managed to bring its own special viciousness to the narrative. Mormons believed Native Americans were a holy offshoot of the biblical Hebrews, and Mormons had also recently been driven from lands they considered sacred. One might, therefore, presume Mormons would feel kinship and empathy for the Shoshone. They didn't.

Mormons took no part in the fighting, but they furnished guides (including the infamous Porter Rockwell) to lead U.S. troops to the Shoshone encampment. And while Mormons received wounded Americans into their homes and celebrated their "victory," similar aid was withheld from the bereft and injured Shoshone. Their butchered dead were left where they lay.

My friend Matt and I were recently discussing this history. He's a native of Cache Valley, his antecedents its early settlers. Matt asked, "Do they know exactly how many Shoshone were killed that day?"

They don't. There are only estimates. Some were calculated by Shoshone survivors on the day of the massacre. Another was issued by the U.S. Army within a few days. Still other estimates were produced years later by reanalyzing contemporaneous evidence.

The most accurate estimate is probably 255 Shoshone slain on the day of the attack, which, according to Madsen, is the number reported to Washington, D.C., by the Shoshone. Other estimates range from 120 up to 1,200, but the Shoshone's own report seems reliable; it would have been a personal accounting of family members and neighbors.

The volunteers' commanding officer, Colonel Patrick E. Connor, reported that his force of just under 200 fighting men killed 224 Shoshone. While Connor might be inclined to overstate his enemy's casualties to embellish his own valor, he evidently based his report strictly on the bodies he personally counted at the site. This overlooks Shoshone who died outside the vicinity, such as those who fell into the Bear River and drowned. It also would not account for Shoshone people who escaped but then perished of exposure, starvation and mortal injuries. Significantly, neither estimate differentiates warriors from civilians. Madsen says ninety women and children were likely among the dead. So, the composition and exact total of Shoshone dead remains unknown.

As I told Matt this, he winced.

I knew that wince. I had effected it myself. It's the wince of White, male Americans on learning of yet another misdeed from our appalling history. Matt and I are also Mormons. He's a faithful, eighth-generation member; I'm devoutly ex-Mormon. I bear the additional onus of being a former enlistee of the U.S. Army—a veritable Yahtzee of the demographically damned.

"Can you imagine coming up on a scene like that?" Matt asked. "Three hundred or so bodies?"

I can't. It's so much easier to just picture the Shoshone going about their lives in the canyons and grasslands of Cache Valley. Imagining the massacre comes uncomfortably close to self-indictment. I've never been forced to do this—the event has never been widely publicized, and White memorials employ comforting falsehoods and misleading language, such as referring to the event as the "Battle of Bear River." Only in the past ten years has its significance been acknowledged and the accepted terminology amended to Bear River Massacre or, more compellingly, Massacre at Boa Ogoi.

History has a way of keeping things to itself, but once it has your attention, it will show you every grisly and distasteful detail and dare you to look away. That's what I was tempted to do when I learned about Connor's deliberately murderous dawn-time raid, how he positioned his men by night, knowing the Shoshone's ability to fight and maneuver would be severely hampered by the presence of women, children and elderly in the middle of winter. At one point, Connor even ordered his men to encircle the encampment and advance from all sides, just like the predator ring hunt.

I wanted to look away from the account of a U.S. soldier who dispensed supposed mercy killings on incapacitated Shoshone by braining them with an axe. And I didn't know what to do with the report of U.S. soldiers who murdered Shoshone women who "would not submit quietly to be ravished" and who raped mortally wounded women as they died.

Darren Parry, former chairman of the Northwestern Band of the Shoshone Nation, is the author of *Bear River Massacre: A Shoshone History*, published in 2020. He puts the Shoshone death toll at 400. This number is based on Shoshone oral tradition, but it seems grimly plausible to add 145 collateral dead to the Shoshone's on-site estimate of 255.

Parry's book contains few historical details about the massacre, but it recounts what happened in the 157 years afterward, which, in some ways, is just as shocking. In the end, the devastated and subdued Northwestern Shoshone threw themselves on the mercy of the Mormons, who offered to teach the Shoshone how to farm and ranch—if they'd be baptized and assimilate into White Mormon society. Accordingly, Parry himself is not only a descendant of the massacre survivors but also a sixth-generation Mormon.

Left: Daughters of the Pioneers plaque at existing Bear River Massacre memorial site.

Below: Darren Parry at 2020 memorial observation of the Bear River Massacre.

So, not all of the Northwestern Shoshone were driven off. Today, many dwell in their sacred Cache Valley, and Parry says they fiercely maintain their cultural identity. The tribe recently purchased a large portion of the massacre site and is at work curating the hallowed ground, constructing a new memorial and interpretive center and accurately presenting the history and its context. Interestingly, the new Shoshone memorial might include restoration of Battle Creek, which could serve as a habitat for native Bonneville cutthroat.

The parallels between the Shoshone's encounter with European invaders and that of the Bear River's wildlife are impossible to dismiss, particularly the fish. Both the native people and trout of the Bear River watershed were unprepared for the foreign onslaught, and both were conquered with disquieting ease by relentless, impassive foes. Fortunately, both also evaded complete extermination, surviving in numbers sufficient to recover and perhaps reclaim their rightful place in the region.

Parry writes, "I am neither angry nor bitter about the treatment of Native Americans in the past, but I am passionate about making sure that our voice is heard in the future." Amazingly, if Parry had any animosity for White people, the United States or the Mormon Church, he has let go of it.

Letting go isn't the problem I have. It'd be a mistake to give up the shame I bear for abuses committed by those whose identity and culture I share. This is especially true for a massacre that occurred on the banks of the river where I retreat from the supposedly civilized world to go fishing, where I catch not only fish but also imagined glimpses of indigenous people and wildlife.

"It's not easy to decide what to do with it," Matt observed, "where to put that shame."

A salient point: as metaphysical as it sounds, shame must be *placed*. Unless it's dismissed, which in this case would seem unjust, shame will *reside* somewhere. Placing it on an individual, on someone's personal identity, gives rise only to self-loathing or false piety, neither of which are benefits to society. If, however, the shame could be shifted onto the history itself, to the Massacre at Boa Ogoi, it might be forced into productivity, to amplify marginalized voices and make it more difficult to forget or repeat such terrible acts.

The namesake of the Bear River is making a comeback. The Utah Division of Wildlife Resources has reported that Utah's bear population has grown slowly but steadily since the 1980s, and there might now be as many as thirty black bears in Cache Valley.

Some years ago, while serving as a Scoutmaster at a campout at Cinnamon Creek, I heard that a couple of my Scouts claimed to have spotted a bear. Under questioning, the first boy confirmed the rumor, but the second confessed he'd only been repeating what the first had said. The first boy then became eager to tell us that whatever it was he'd seen, it had been at a great remove or, as he put it, "really way far away."

We Scout leaders traded dubious looks, but the possibility of a bear in the vicinity was at once problematic and intriguing, so we mounted an earnest search. We saw no bears, nor any sign of bears, but we kept searching until it was late. As the sky grew dark, we headed back to camp, glancing over our shoulders as we went.

6.

DEAR FEBRUARY

Dear February,
It's time to be honest.
I don't love you.
I never did.

It's not because you're cold. December is cold, but she and I get along just fine. January is even colder, and moody, but she and I get along great.

Your cold is different. Your cold feels intentional. Spiteful.

Maybe it's the way you mope around in that ratty gray bathrobe of leftover snow. Or how you paint the sky with colorless gloom, transforming each week into one vast overcast Tuesday.

We don't have much in common. I'm interested in fly-fishing, and you're into dead presidents and clairvoyant rodents. Your effect on freestone streams is a huge turnoff. By the time you show up, the easy fishing of autumn is a memory, and even the brown trout spawn has been over for eight weeks. The Blacksmith Fork salmonfly hatch is out there, somewhere, but it's keeping its distance, like my buddy who avoids me because he says my girlfriend is crazy.

I'm aware of your backwater midge hatches on the lower Logan. And, yeah, I see those little black snowflies of yours throughout the watershed. Hell, you might even warm up one day and show me some surprise mayflies at Black Canyon. That's nice. But don't let's kid ourselves—the next day you'll be bitter again, which makes things worse.

Even when you're nice, you're mean.

Last year I caught two fish during your entire stay. That's all. Two brown trout on the Logan River. The first was dozing at the bottom of a

Left: Mink Creek brook trout.

Below: Cub River at Willow Flat.

Salmonfly adult. *Courtesy of Kyle Jensen.*

Brad Hansen. *Courtesy of Brad Hansen.*

Left: A fluvial Bonneville cutthroat trout of the Bear River watershed.

Below: Bloomington Lake.

Left: Blacksmith Fork.

Below: Cub River at Willow Flat. *Courtesy of Klaus VanZanten.*

Right: Paul
Thompson.
*Courtesy of Tyler
Coleman.*

Below: Middle
Basin near Ryder
Lake, Uinta
Mountains.

Andrew Engel. *Courtesy of Andrew Engel.*

Bear River.

Left: Chadd VanZanten.
Courtesy of Brad Hansen.

Below: Tyler Coleman.
Courtesy of Tyler Coleman.

Right: The brunette
paramour.

Below: Blacksmith
Fork brown trout.
Courtesy of Kyle Jensen.

Left: Jim DeRito. *Courtesy of Tyler Coleman.*

Below: Jason Reed.

Bear River
at Oneida
Narrows.

Blacksmith Fork at Trespass Flats.

Right: Russ Beck.

Below: Ryder Lake,
Uinta Mountains.

Trespass Flats Bonneville cutthroat trout.

Bill Kramer.

Left: Cub River.

Below: Donicio Gomez. *Courtesy of Jesse Males.*

Little Bear River.

Logan River.

Left: Logan River at Denzil Stewart Nature Park.

Below: Blacksmith Fork at Trespass Flats.

Left: Cinnamon Creek.

Below: Middle Basin of the Uinta Mountains.

Little Bear River.

deep scour in a bend. I saw him down there, miserable in the crystalline baseflow, barely twitching. He bit the size-12 Surveyor I sank down to him but not until I'd moved the strike indicator all the way up the tippet and then halfway up the leader and finally onto the flyline—and practically plonked him on the snout with the fly.

The second brown ate a microscopic Zebra Midge with no strike indicator in a slow backwater, but the take was so timid and ambivalent that the hook only just snagged the translucent scrim of skin on the outside of his upper lip. At any other time of the year, that fish would've shaken the hook, but the water was probably thirty-nine degrees, and the little brown fought like a tranquilized kitten.

This year's been a little better. I caught a few decent whitefish that chased down a dead-drifted Woolly Bugger. I appreciated that. But even when you get me into a double-digit count, I go home with aching fingers and nostrils frozen. You treat the trout bad—they're half-starved, listless, heads inclining to the streambed as though praying for March. They're as sick of you as I am.

A fishing pal of mine slipped on the ice and hurt his back not long after you got here, and he missed fishing this past weekend. Not that there was much to miss—a few foot-long browns up at Twin Bridges, a ten-inch cutthroat or two. As I scrabbled up and down the long, steep banks, perilously half-snow, half-mudslide, I pictured my laid-up buddy at his tying vise, warm pink fingers working a bobbin at a relaxed pace. Or just reading a book. His wife passes by and sets down something hot for him to sip. She pats his shoulder, glad to have him in the house on a Saturday.

I actually envy his excuse to stay in. That's how bad it's gotten. But you whine: "You never take me anywhere." I know you won't put out, but the phrase "you never know" gets murmured a lot just before fishing trips in February. So, I go.

And you're as icy as ever.

You have your good days, yes. I get Presidents' Day off, but what's there to do? Go fishing? And Groundhog Day is so dull it makes Arbor Day seem like Halloween in Tijuana. I suppose you catch the occasional Mardi Gras, but Lent starts the very next day, which actually suits you better.

No surprise that your big moment is Valentine's Day—that most fraught and imperious annual observance when we gentleman anglers can't fish at all but must lay aside our flyrods to tremble through lace-trimmed rituals, pen clumsy penances into saccharine greeting cards and purchase heart-shaped boxes of chocolate indulgences.

I'm aware that this might not be all your fault. You're a neglected, unappreciated month, relegated to the ass-end of winter with a name that's seldom even pronounced properly. Centuries ago, somebody bilked you out of two whole days to compensate for the solar system's disregard for the 365-day Gregorian calendar. I half suspect this was a scheme hatched by anglers

Logan River.

to transfer two perfectly good fishing days to a better, warmer month, so it's no wonder you're frigid.

More and more often, you bring rain to the West and here to the Bear River. Twenty years ago, your grip was positively arctic, and you weren't such a crybaby. Your precipitation was often just swarms of ice crystals that did not so much fall but instead hung on the motionless air, landing on the skin like the touch of a needle's tip. But now climate change has overtaken you like menopause, and you cry maudlin tears at the drop of a hat.

This watershed needs rain, but it's a matter of timing, Feb. Rain in late March and April is welcome. Rain in the middle of winter, which melts snowpack and swells streams, can be catastrophic—not only to humans with homes in a floodplain but also to fish whose migration and spawning are keyed to a more predictable hydrograph.

So, it's not like I don't see your side of things. I do. You know I feel bad when Leap Year throws off your twenty-eight-day cycle, and I always correct those who misspell your name.

But you can see my side, too: one day last winter while you were hanging around, I scared up a solitary trout from under a pile of driftwood stacked in a bend at DeWitt Spring. The poor creature fled about three feet and then stopped cold, as if to say, "On second thought, just kill me. It'll save me from another two weeks of February."

So, I'm sorry, but I'm through fishing with you. I can say "you never know" only so many times before I realize that I actually do. Time to face it—you might be the shortest month, but baby, you're the longest too.

7.

A TALE OF TWO DAMS

There are seven major dams on the Bear River, along with dozens of other smaller dams and diversions, and there are more than one hundred dams on the Bear River's tributaries. This watershed is infested with dams.

This is the tale of two of them.

The first is Cove Dam, completed in 1917 on the Bear River, downstream from Black Canyon in Idaho. It's one in a series of dams on the Bear constructed in the early 1900s for irrigation, flood control and hydroelectricity. Cove Dam, Soda Dam, Grace Dam and Oneida Dam were collectively known as the Bear River Project.

By 1917, the development of the Bear River was well underway. The first claim to Bear River water for irrigation was already over fifty years old (filed in Wyoming in 1862), and the Bear's first big dam was pushing thirty (Wheelon Dam, constructed in Utah in 1889).

But the Bear River Project represented a new, more industrial approach to water development. The project eventually boasted a combined installed capacity of seventy-seven megawatts. That doesn't sound like much today (by comparison, Hoover Dam's installed capacity is 2,080 megawatts). However, at the time, the *Salt Lake Herald* gushed that the Bear River Project was "the greatest development of hydraulic power between the Mississippi and California rivers."

In 1989, the Bear River Project, including Cove Dam, was acquired by energy titan PacifiCorp. In 1996, it came time for PacifiCorp to renew its Bear

River operating licensing with the Federal Energy Regulatory Commission (FERC). When FERC floated the idea of PacifiCorp repairing at least some of the harm the four dams had inflicted, PacifiCorp balked, asserting that that damage was done long before it arrived.

The company was right. The impacts from stacking four dams on forty miles of river were severe and prolonged. For example, Cove Dam was more than a mile from its own power plant—the water was conveyed from the forebay to generators by aboveground flowlines that circumvented the river entirely. Grace Dam was over five miles from its power plant. Together, these flowlines left more than eight miles of bypassed Bear River essentially dewatered for eighty-eight years.

I spoke about this to my fishing buddy Ken Theis. A laconic Coloradan, Ken is bespectacled and sober but quite witty. He was an environmental consultant ("insultant," as he put it) on PacifiCorp's relicensing.

"That whole stretch of river had been written off ecologically," he began.

But despite PacifiCorp's objections, FERC conditioned the relicensing on conducting studies and implementing mitigation to offset the ecological impacts and neglect. PacifiCorp had no choice but to comply.

"We thought, with objective, science-based studies," said Ken, "maybe we can get a little more water into the channel, maybe reconnect some spawning habitat. That'd help the few native cutthroats that might remain."

Ken said PacifiCorp's position was that there were no Bonneville cutthroats in that part of the Bear—only agency-stocked put-and-take rainbow trout—so why bother with fisheries studies? "Dick Scully," Ken continued, "regional fisheries manager for Idaho Fish and Game at the time, said, 'Maybe there aren't any Bonnevilles in there, but there should be!'"

Then, one day, Ken made an important discovery.

"We were doing flow measurements at Cove," Ken told me, "and I saw a few fish rising in the bypass channel where spring flow maintained a few pools in the reach that was normally dewatered. So, I went back later with my flyrod and caught a couple twelve-inch trout. They were cutthroats. Nobody knew there were any cutts left. Once I convinced Idaho Fish and Game, that's really when things changed."

However, three years later, PacifiCorp and FERC still had no licensing agreement, and PacifiCorp was squirming out of the studies it had committed to.

"Doing actual science would have revealed the full extent of those historic impacts," explained Ken, "which might've led to more mitigation requirements. PacifiCorp didn't want that. They wanted to maintain the status quo. So, they devised alternative, subjective studies. The objective, baseline studies never got done."

Challenged by resource agencies and the public, FERC and PacifiCorp formed a compromise settlement. Instead of conducting studies to assess the river's condition, PacifiCorp agreed to a range of projects to benefit the river and the newly discovered cutthroats, while maintaining its power-generation revenues.

First, PacifiCorp agreed to release water from Grace Dam into the bypass reach of the Bear. These releases were initially conceived to mimic annual spring runoff and improve riverine conditions, but they devolved into "boater flows," a concession to kayakers—peak-flows released on weekends in spring and summer that transform Black Canyon into Class 5 whitewater that attracts kayakers from all over the country.

Ken says this does nothing for the fishery. "Those flows are about as natural as a theme park water slide."

PacifiCorp also agreed to reroute spring flows that would no longer be used for power generation. According to a plan Ken developed, fifteen cubic feet per second of spring flow was redirected into the Bear via an abandoned river channel. Known as Kackley Spring, its sparkling clear flow now forms a two-mile tributary of the often-turbid Bear. A fish ladder permits only Bonneville cutthroats into the creek, and it's the site of annual cutthroat spawning.

Quite monumentally, during the settlement negotiations of 2002, Ken raised the prospect of removing Cove Dam entirely. Faced with FERC requirements to provide expensive fish passage, PacifiCorp conceded to relinquishing the meager revenue generated by the dilapidated Cove Dam. The removal was completed in 2006, reconnecting thirty miles of the mainstem channel now known to harbor native cutthroats.

It is the first and only time a major, modern dam has been removed from the Bear River. So, the first of the two dams in this tale is one that no longer exists.

The second dam is one conceived by the Twin Lakes Canal Company (TLCC), proposed for construction on the Bear River in Idaho in the early 2000s. If approved, it would be the first major new dam on the Bear River since the 1920s. There could not have been many people still alive who'd witnessed such an event, and at first, the proposal received little attention. (That didn't last.)

The justification for the dam was not preposterous—TLCC claimed it needed more water for its customers. Clair Bosen, TLCC's president, said

Above: Bear River at Cove Dam site, 1968. *Courtesy of U.S. Library of Congress.*

Opposite: Bear River at Cove Dam site, 2020.

the project would also generate electricity, strengthen the local economy and provide recreation just as good as the river ever had. He even promised to transmit the water in pipes, rather than wasteful open canals.

"It's not good just for the Twin Lakes Canal Company," Bosen burbled. "It's something that's good for the entire county."

In 2006, TLCC filed documents with FERC for preliminary permission to erect the dam and a year later applied to the Idaho Department of Water Resources for water rights to fill it up.

However, now that the proposal was public, opposition was immediate and strenuous.

Evidently, nobody cared about enriching the local economy or the virtues of piped irrigation. The bone of contention was the proposed location—the Oneida Narrows section of the Bear River, a picturesque canyon where five miles of the river flowed over boulder-strewn substrates between scenic cliff walls and pockets of verdant meadow. Locals—not just fly anglers—were hopelessly in love with the place. The Narrows held big browns and rainbows ranging from sixteen to twenty-two inches, but

apparently, inner-tubing down the river was the activity most protestors were really desperate to preserve.

The Bear River was also already crammed with dams. Cutler Dam was forty miles downstream from the proposed site, and there were no fewer than four major dams within forty miles upstream. In fact, the nearest dam was only five miles upstream—Oneida Reservoir. The water in TLCC's new dam would rise practically to the spillway of the old one.

I first heard about the controversy from my friend Star Coulbrooke. Sprightly and petite, Star was an unreformed hippie boomer with the punk-rock bohemian flamboyance of a singer in an electric folk band—tattoos, spiky hair, alarming accumulations of jewelry. A poet and protégé of Ken Brewer, Star wrote passionate verse about the legends, scandals and waterways of southeastern Idaho. She was also a native of Preston, the small, sleepy Idaho town just miles from the Narrows, where she had probably tubed more than anyone. Star said she'd once counted 127 people lazily floating the Narrows during a single Friday afternoon.

Bear River at Oneida Narrows.

Many groups rose up to fight the proposed dam, including Bear Lake Watch, Bear River Watershed Council, Great Salt Lake Keeper, Greater Yellowstone Coalition, Idaho Rivers United and Trout Unlimited, but Star's Preston-based grassroots group, the Oneida Narrows Organization, led the charge.

Star's argument was simple: Oneida Narrows was one of the last unspoiled, free-flowing sections of the Bear, and it would be immoral to allow Clair Bosen to drown it. At every protest rally, on every petition, she repeated it: "The last free-flowing section of the Bear." It was her battle cry.

It was also completely misleading.

In reality, most of Oneida Narrows had been underwater for nearly one hundred years—beneath the seven-mile-long Oneida Reservoir. The river running through the remaining four miles of the Narrows was not free flowing; it was the tailwater of the Oneida Reservoir, and the fly-fishing there was fantastic, but after exiting the Narrows, the Bear flowed brown and sullen through forty miles of hardcore ag land before terminating in Cutler Reservoir, arguably the most impaired waterway in the watershed.

You'd never want to inner-tube down a free-flowing Bear River. It would be treacherous and mercurial, its channel migrating and hydrograph whipsawing between deafening springtime flows of ten thousand cubic feet per second and drought-like trickles that might not sustain an antelope herd.

But even though the idea of a free-flowing river at Oneida Narrows was a myth, it actually made TLCC's proposal more tragic. It was as if the energy developers would not be happy until the entire river was dammed and developed.

In 2007, Star and her partner, Mitch Butterfield, began an unremitting assault on TLCC and Clair Bosen. Star outmaneuvered them in the press. She out-organized them in Preston. She testified at hearings, filed objections, organized rallies, read her poetry to crowds and encouraged everyone to join the struggle.

This went on for five years.

In a single month, she collected 1,748 signatures on a petition opposing the dam. An online petition collected almost 800 more. This in a county with a total population of just 12,000. It seemed like public opinion was dead set against the dam.

"When Mitch and I first created the petition," Star told me, "we took it around to the Preston Night Rodeo, and people practically tore it out of our hands to sign it."

In 2012, Clair Bosen was still expressing confidence that he'd win the day, but he sometimes seemed a little rattled: "Our company has spent over $2.5 million on studies that were required by Fish and Game and Trout Unlimited and so on, to study the fish and the birds and the bats and the bees and the rabbits and the snails and the deer and elk, moose and eagles, and anything you can think of."

In October 2012, the Idaho Department of Water Resources denied TLCC's water-right application, meaning TLCC now had no way to fill the reservoir, even if FERC approved its construction. And so when Clair Bosen filed the full dam construction application with FERC anyhow, it proved that the dam was a foregone conclusion all along, a pre-wired backroom deal.

Star said, "You get a final document that says you've won, but the victory is tenuous. If someone can make money, they'll find a new way to get around the last denial."

Another four years passed before the final blow landed. In 2016, FERC rejected TLCC's application to construct the dam. There was no pre-wiring after all. The fight was over. According to FERC's terrifyingly thorough environmental impact statement, there were numerous reasons for the

Oneida Narrows rainbow trout.

rejection, but it came down to TLCC's inability "to adequately offset the adverse effects of constructing and operating a new major hydroelectric project on a currently scenic river reach in an undeveloped canyon with remarkable recreational, geological, and wildlife values and public access."

Not even the federal government could stand to inundate a place with such fabulous inner-tubing.

"We cried and laughed and scoffed at the would-be dammers and wrote poems," said Star. "We floated the river and dreamed of the river and fell in love with the river over and over again."

So, the dams in this tale are the only two in the watershed that do not exist—one removed, and the other never approved. Sadly, there aren't many free-flowing rivers anymore, anywhere. They were given up more than a century ago by people who didn't know better and could not have guessed that they were leaving us to skirmish over stubby sections of stream that only slightly resemble the way they once were.

8.

THE YEAR I GOT IT RIGHT

All flyboxes are endowed with one mysterious property: you can only ever find the one you don't really need at the moment. I reaffirmed this one morning in late March as I searched in vain for the flybox with all my salmonfly patterns in it. I needed it so I could do something I'd never done before, something I'd been putting off, something I needed to get right.

It was time once and for all to own the Blacksmith Fork salmonfly hatch.

It shouldn't have been difficult to find the flybox; I'd never owned very many. Most of my angler friends had lots more than I did, like multiple dozens—flyboxes for every fly type and for individual patterns. My fly-tying mentor, Tim King, surely had more than he could easily list stacked around his tying bench like books of arcane lore in the medieval laboratory of an alchemist.

I'd fished the Blacksmith Fork salmonfly hatch before, sometimes catching lots of fish and sometimes not. Either way, it usually felt like I'd simply showed up on the right or wrong day. This time I wanted to make a plan, be systematic. This would be the year I got it right.

I told Russ Beck about this nutty idea to fish with the benefit of forethought, rather than my usual habit of blundering into the water at random times and places.

"I'll go with you," he replied with some urgency. He'd never properly plundered the salmonfly hatch, either. "Let's go tomorrow."

"Nah," I said. "It's way too early. And I'm fishing mostly during the week, anyway, when no one's around. I'm scheduling time off from work. I got a plan. I'm gonna dial this thing in."

As in many western freestone rivers, the salmonfly population of the Blacksmith Fork consists of mainly the giant salmonfly (*Pteronarcys californica*) and the least salmonfly (*Pteronarcella badia*). Both are biotic indicator species, meaning they're so intolerant of water impurities that their mere presence indicates high-quality water and habitat. Significantly, their absence indicates the opposite.

Salmonflies are just very large stoneflies, so their life cycle is much like that of their smaller cousins. In their larval life stage, salmonflies are called "naiads"—detritus shredders that cling to the undersides of rocks in clear, swift freestone systems. Resembling nothing so much as tiny dragons, salmonfly naiads are dark brown, scaly and two inches long or longer. In the spring of their third or fourth year, they make synchronous migrations to the streambanks to emerge, usually at night. Their cast-off skins, known as exuviae, remain on the rocks and trees like ghosts. Adults might be three inches long, covered with blue-black carapace over salmon-colored bodies, which gives rise to their common name. Their slender, darkly veined wings look like miniature cathedral windows glazed into reticulations of heavy black iron. After baking their exoskeletons in sunlight, they take wing with the flight characteristics of overloaded cargo choppers. Somehow knowing that their eggs will be swept downstream, salmonflies make compensatory upstream sorties to more accurately target their natal streambeds. After mating, females divebomb the water, releasing fertilized egg masses, which accrete at the ends of their abdomens.

It'd be difficult to overstate the importance of salmonflies as a prey item for freestone trout. They're fat and heavy, hundreds of times larger than other aquatic insects. A couple of handfuls would, in a pinch, make a decent meal for your average-sized fly angler.

Unlike salmonfly hatches on legendary rivers like the Madison or Deschutes, Blacksmith Fork's salmonfly hatch doesn't last six weeks. Nor does it span twenty river miles, and the insects don't always emerge in horror show profusions. Instead, the Blacksmith Fork salmonfly hatch can be furtive and fleeting. It's like spiraling a football through a small window, the opening of which you'll miss if you don't pay attention.

I finally found the flybox. Inside, there were three kinds of flies. Those that had been in there the longest looked like preserved museum specimens, boasting authentic-looking wings, the correct number of abdominal

Salmonfly naiad. *Courtesy of Kyle Jensen.*

segments and legs akimbo at anatomically precise angles. They were the expensive flies I'd purchased when I first started chasing salmonflies. Back then, I got all my advice from the dude at the flyshop, who, of course, always ushered me to the premium fly bins.

"These're the flies that'll really catch fish," he purred. "See the detail? Look at those wings. These trout're smart. They know the difference. Now, you pick out a dozen nymphs and a dozen adults, and I'll go start the paperwork for your financing."

The flies placed into the salmonfly box in the previous couple years were those I'd tied myself, hence they were lopsided and unsightly. They bore a passing likeness to the natural, and they caught fish, but because my tying skills were poor, and they took so long to tie, I would grow fonder and fonder of each one until I was too sentimentally attached to waste them on fish.

Fortunately, there was a third kind of fly in my stash: the impressionistic, less-pricey, shop-tied salmonfly patterns I'd started buying after I quit listening to the shop dude. These included the Carburetor, invented by the aforementioned Tim King, who often named fly patterns after whatever part of his venerable VW Bug he happened to be rebuilding at the time. The Carburetor pattern was preceded by the Alternator and followed by the Regulator. (Hopefully, he's never reduced to inventing a fly called the Thrown Tie Rod.)

A handful of Pat's Rubber Legs would suffice to imitate the nymph, so the year I got it right commenced.

Fishing salmonflies on a big western river is an exercise in locating the hatch advancing upstream, choosing locally successful fly patterns and slingshot casting up under the brush. On the big waters, it's mainly about tactics.

The Blacksmith Fork salmonfly hatch is largely a *strategic* undertaking—less about perfecting your slingshot cast and more about patience and record keeping (but bring your slingshot game too). The Blacksmith Fork hatch has lots of moving parts and mutually exclusive conditions. Luck involves itself to a greater extent than many anglers are comfortable with.

The first complication is timing. Blacksmith Fork salmonflies might appear any time between mid-April and June but predicting exactly when would be about as easy as figuring out Colonel Sanders's Original Recipe by sniffing the air while driving past a KFC.

Next, rather than the typical duration of six weeks or longer, the entire Blacksmith Fork salmonfly hatch lasts three weeks at the outside and sometimes only two. Once underway, the hatch moves upstream at speeds that vary between imperceptible and wait, it's over?

Compound all of this with the excellent likelihood that the hatch overlaps or indeed synchronizes with the dangerously high flows of spring runoff, which might prohibit fishing the hatch altogether. So, it's more like spiraling a football through several windows at once, windows that might swing open or closed at different times.

That's why, instead of circling a few days on my calendar, I blocked out an open-ended range of days spanning half of April, the first of which should fall too early to see any salmonflies at all. That way, I'd already be fishing when the hatch began.

I checked the United States Geological Survey (USGS) flow reports to ensure the probability of drowning in the Blacksmith Fork spring runoff was acceptably moderate and then I scheduled a series of prospecting trips roughly every other day for the following couple of weeks.

Blacksmith Fork Canyon is narrow, as canyons go. Its walls loom over the river, the rocky bed of which winds through pockets of forest. For my first prospecting trip, I went to the mouth of the canyon and waded along the banks, overturning submerged rocks and rifling the brush. I found salmonfly nymphs but no adults. Using a big Carburetor as a strike indicator and a weighted Rubber Legs to imitate migrating nymphs that'd lost their footing, I hit the brushiest edges of the diciest falls and riffles. I was hoping for underwhelming results, which would suggest the nymphs were not yet on the march. In two hours of fishing, just one small brown trout took my dry and one large whitefish took my nymph. Good, I thought, the baseline. I charted this on a sheet of graph paper in terms of catch per hour.

The next few outings were similar—no conspicuous interest in either fly. It was odd to be so pleased at catching no fish. A couple of weeks later, however, trout were reliably responding to the nymph. I made more dots on my graph paper, and they formed an upward-trending line.

Between trips, I remained focused on what I now referred to as "The Project," avoiding friends and anything else that might interfere, such as my job and the family I was raising at the time. At the start of the third week, I saw adult salmonflies and exuvial castings stuck to the rocks in groups of two and three. As I plotted my latest data, the line inclined.

There were setbacks. One day I strayed too far upstream and fished with disappointing results. Then one of my children had a birthday, so I could only fish part of that day. Also, the flows started coming up, and I fell down and barked my shin pretty badly in a pushy current.

Worst of all were the numerous other anglers. The Project schedule stuck mostly to weekdays explicitly to avoid weekenders, but I knew the flyshop dude would be hawking fistfuls of lifelike, high-dollar salmonfly patterns and directing entire convoys of anglers into Blacksmith Fork Canyon every single day between Groundhog Day and the Fourth of July. I'd been grifted that way myself many years before, and later I worked at the fly shop and saw the con from the opposite end.

This is the final and most aggravating complication. The canyon section of the Blacksmith Fork is only fifteen miles long to begin with, and the salmonfly hatch is most conspicuous in the lower five. So, a dozen fly anglers fresh from the premium fly bins were all it took to instantly set the lower Blacksmith Fork to full capacity.

But despite the crowds and perilous currents, the dots and lines told the tale. The Project stood on the verge of a breakthrough. I was finally plumbing the true fecundity of the Blacksmith Fork salmonfly hatch.

What I haven't mentioned yet is that the truly puzzling mystery of the hatch is not how to successfully fly-fish it. The bigger enigma—perhaps the most elusive ecological question of the entire Bear River watershed—is why *californica* and *badia* salmonflies are found in the Blacksmith Fork but not in the Logan River, which lies just ten miles to the north.

Historically referred to as June bugs, salmonflies used to inhabit the Logan River. In a 1927 paper, naturalist James Needham reported that *californica* and *badia* were abundant in the Logan. This makes perfect sense—the Logan River and Blacksmith Fork both drain the western slope of the Bear River Mountains, they're nearly identical in terms of high-quality habitat and water and the Logan has more of both. Indeed, the Blacksmith Fork is a tributary to the Logan River, emptying into the Logan five miles east of the Logan's confluence with the Little Bear River.

Yet the last collection of salmonflies from the Logan River occurred in 1966, by master's student Nancy Erman, and haven't been collected from the Logan since.

In 1994, the National Aquatic Monitoring Center at Utah State University, a highly respected aquatic research unit known as the Bug Lab, remarked that salmonflies were absent from the Logan River, but it was not until 2000 that it learned the insects had once been common there, so for more than thirty years, the mystery itself lay undiscovered. The Bug Lab soon launched a quest to find out why the Logan had no salmonflies and what could be done about it.

First, researchers examined all available science to make sure they'd not overlooked any post-1966 reports of Logan River salmonflies. They hadn't. Bug Lab director Mark Vinson also made damn sure there really were no

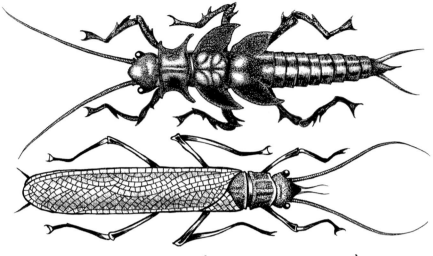

GIANT SALMONFLY *(PTERONARCYS CALIFORNICA)*

salmonflies in the Logan—between 1992 and 2004, he made more than two hundred sampling trips to that river without finding a single salmonfly.

There were a couple of sketchy theories about what might have happened. One early supposition was that there had been some sort of chemical release in the Logan River around 1966. Suspects included herbicides thought to have been used by the Utah Department of Transportation for sagebrush eradication along U.S. Highway 89 through Logan Canyon. Another was road deicing agents that might have spilled into the river, which flows close to the highway in many places.

But these guesses couldn't bear scrutiny. For one thing, research revealed no such historical environmental incidents. Moreover, if a toxic release were to blame, surely it would have dissipated since the 1960s. However, the word *baffling* was chosen by Bug Lab personnel to describe the salmonflies' complete failure to naturally recolonize the Logan.

"Salmonflies are not the best fliers," reported Vinson, "so dispersal would likely be slow, but after forty years they should have made some inroads into the Logan River."

In fact, salmonflies were present in the Blacksmith Fork just upstream from its confluence with the Logan River, so recolonizing their former range would presumably require very little effort, but salmonflies were not found upstream or downstream from the confluence, nor anywhere else in the Logan.

Okay, they said, what about a long-term, ongoing pollution source in the Logan River? This was as historically groundless as the previous theories and ignored the reality that the Logan River is still home to other, equally sensitive biotic indicator species (like the golden stonefly), which would necessarily be as negatively impacted as salmonflies but were not.

Without a reason why the Logan shouldn't make a good home to salmonflies, the Bug Lab decided to recolonize the insects itself. Vinson had already experimented with the idea in 2001 by placing Blacksmith Fork salmonfly nymphs in plastic tubes anchored to the bottom of the Logan River. One of his nymphs survived for more than a year. In 2004, Vinson developed an annual transplant program of a more wholesale nature. In an insect recolonization campaign said to be the first of its kind, dozens of volunteers brought everything from kick nets to butterfly nets to capture tens of thousands of Blacksmith Fork salmonflies for relocation in the Logan River.

To those of us without scientific training, this seemed like a great idea—put the salmonflies in the Logan, and they'll flourish. Because we all knew that introducing only a few specimens of a nonnative species into an unsuspecting biome was a surefire way to not only colonize them but also set off their explosive growth. Bringing thousands of salmonflies to a river where they were already natives was a no-brainer. Local newspapers ran headlines like "Return of the Salmonfly," as though they'd already returned.

But they didn't return.

In 2005, a few *californica* exuviae and two young-of-year nymphs were collected from the Logan River, but further evidence of transplanting success was never found. The program was a favorite among area volunteers and was featured in *TROUT Magazine* in winter 2005, but the Bug Lab could not justify taking so many salmonflies if they were, as it appeared, perishing by the thousands in the Logan.

Shortly after Vinson left the Bug Lab in 2008, the program was scuttled. The giant salmonfly and least salmonfly are still missing from Logan River.

"It's a mystery that continues to haunt me," Vinson told me.

It's since been shown that Left Hand Fork and the upper reaches of Rock Creek are also absent of salmonflies. This deepens the mystery and adds considerable insult to injury, because both of those streams are first-order tributaries to the Blacksmith Fork.

None of this sits very well with local fly anglers. Logan River is home to the largest self-sustaining population of native Bear River Bonneville cutthroat trout, and until the 1960s, salmonflies must have been a substantial

Salmonfly larvae captured for relocation in Logan River.

part of their diet. The salmonfly's disappearance is just one of numerous ecological indignities suffered by the Bear River cutthroat since the arrival of European settlers, and the salmonfly's return would be of inestimable value. Instead, their absence from the Logan River feels like some curse that we had no way to prevent but have nevertheless inherited. Whoever is responsible for making the Logan River hostile to the salmonflies can never be held to account, and if the storied Bug Lab couldn't bring the salmonflies back, then who can?

This is why fly anglers of the Bear River watershed might secretly feel melancholy or resentful, even after sensational fishing during a salmonfly hatch on the Blacksmith Fork. The only thing I really got right that year was discovering the true value of the salmonflies—not to fly anglers and not just to the trout, but as a reminder that we humans have a nasty habit of inadvertently bumping off entire ecologies, even triggering an "insect apocalypse," and then failing to notice until it's too late to repair it or even understand how it happened.

The Project was a smashing success.

After nearly four weeks of reconnaissance, the dots and lines on my tattered, water-stained graph paper described a curve that was angular but obscenely bulged and simple to interpret: I was fishing the fattest, meatiest period of the salmonfly hatch. The bugs emerged daily and swarmed in the afternoons. The trout were so glutted that they expectorated salmonflies and salmonfly parts. As I jostled the riverside brush, the salmonflies dropped onto me so numerously that I eventually quit noticing the eerie sensation of their hooked feet and exceptionally strong legs pulling and stretching the skin of my neck and scalp.

I threw out my schedule and fished whenever possible—and also when impossible. Before work, after work, instead of work. My boss shot me crusty glances and dropped trenchant comments about job security into everyday conversation. I'd shirk housework and family time for a chance to fish the hatch for just thirty or forty minutes, during which time I might catch twenty good fish. I even rebuffed my wife's rather insistent sexual overtures—an enticement that rarely misfired. What use had I for sex? I was averaging thirty fish an hour in a seething wet arthropod orgy. I'd become Lord of the Salmonflies, King of the *Californicators*.

And then it was over.

I couldn't predict it—at some point I'd discarded the graph paper and just fished. But I didn't need data to notice when the salmonflies quit hatching. The fish kept biting salmonfly patterns for another week, but then they lost interest, and I pictured the line on my graph angling downward to meet the x-axis.

So, I returned to my office, patched things up at home and when the hatch began again the following year, I didn't go up Blacksmith Fork Canyon even once.

There was a day in the middle of it, at the center of The Project, when I had fished out the light, and I sat on the tailgate of my truck, ready to shuck my waders but without the energy to go through with it. The river lay in shadow beneath the high-flung canyon walls, but horizontal shafts of sunlight shot through the upper air of the canyon's narrow mouth, which gives onto the west. Suspended in this carmine glow, the final salmonflies of the day moved as one upriver against a downcanyon breeze. I wondered if one or two of these might blow off course and into the Logan to begin the work of recolonization, or if maybe their offspring would.

The salmonflies flew overhead, hundreds of them, thirty or forty yards high. They made no sound, but I imagined that I could hear them, and the sound was the thrumming of airplane engines, like flak-harried C-130 troop carriers flying in slow formations into the dusk over hostile country.

9

LIGHTS OUT AT WILLARD BAY

Donicio and I really ought to fish together more often. We've known each other for years, live in the same town and get along passably well. We could meet up and within an hour be fishing the Logan or Blacksmith Fork. But we almost never do.

It might be that our philosophies are different: Donicio doesn't have much use for fish under about thirty inches long, and I don't have much use for streams more than about thirty miles away.

When I mention John Gierach's notion that "windshield time" should never exceed the amount of fishing time, Donicio denounces me. "Dude, do *not* listen to that dude!" He wags a finger at me. "That's bullshit! I've driven three hours to fish for one! Like, three hours one way. If there's hot fishing, I'll drive twelve hours. I'll drive all night."

I'm partial to my homewaters, the freestone streams of the Bear River watershed. I take field trips to far-off fisheries of the West's fabled destination waters but not weekly.

Donicio, on the other hand, seems endlessly beguiled by legendary rivers and big fish. He prefers the high-stakes tables almost to the exclusion of local nickel slots. Donicio's a guide, too, so whenever I bump into him, he's always hurrying off to some fabulous location he's not at liberty to discuss in any great detail. Whether guiding or fishing, he's in perpetual pursuit of the next epic trip, the next thirty-inch trout. Donicio's a high roller.

"All or nothing," he proclaims. "Lotta people don't like that style of fishing, but it's always fun."

Willard Bay inlet canal.

I think Donicio is in his mid-forties, but his appearance suggests mid-thirties. His face is boyish, and he's always laughing. He's one of the few people I know who is actually, honestly jolly. He throws trips together on hilariously short notice—or maybe that's only when inviting me. One time he invited me on a two-day fishing trip with six hours of notice. The time before that, he gave me four. I'm always telling him no.

However, a fishing trip is occasionally in the cards for Donicio and me, and one evening in early April found us driving to Willard Bay. I don't mention this to Donicio, but Willard Bay doesn't seem like his kind of fishing. It lacks the glamour of his more typical fishing haunts—the Henry's Fork, the Green, the Blackfoot—or farther afield in Canada and Costa Rica.

Willard Bay just doesn't compare. It's a human-made, fifteen-square-mile freshwater reservoir situated on the east side of the Great Salt Lake, surrounded by an unkempt patchwork of former ag lands and pastures turned wild. The bay is bordered by U.S. Interstate 15 on one side and muddy backwaters on the other. Along one shoreline, giant steel-girder transmission towers stand in an endless rank like robot sentinels in a story by H.G. Wells. There's just not much natural grandeur here. No one would ever mistake it for something like a lake, let alone a bay. With its linear, treeless dikes, it looks less like a reservoir and more like a vast industrial settling pond. But like many low-rent, ersatz waterways, Willard Bay is full of nonnative fish, a warm water angler's wet dream. It's stocked with bluegill, bullhead, catfish, crappie, smallmouth, walleye (with a twenty-four-inch slot limit) and the species it's famous for: the wiper.

A laboratory hybrid of striped bass and white bass, wipers are tall-bodied fish, and they mature into powerful fighters. Donicio tells me wiper season is fast approaching, if not like already seriously *here*. He says when the wipers roll on the surface to feed on spawning shad, they're highly susceptible to streamers.

"If they're up on the banks," Donicio explains, shaking his head gravely, "it's lights out, man. It's bam, bam, bam." With each *bam* he sets an imaginary hook on an imaginary wiper with his imaginary rod.

That's one thing I admire about Donicio: he's always 100 percent sure the next trip is going to be outrageously successful, an assumption based on little more than his intentions to fish there. His optimism has neither practical limits nor grounding in reality.

We pull into the parking lot of a big army surplus store. Before continuing, Donicio says, we're meeting someone, a young guy who wants to guide for the same outfitter where Donicio works. The trip is doubling as the kid's job interview. "My boss wants me to check him out. You know, see if he knows his shit."

The kid is waiting for us. He gets out of his truck, and diffident introductions take place there on the asphalt. The kid looks like a guide: skinny, mid-twenties, tanned brown as a wallet, untrimmed beard. The Chacos, the baggy long-sleeved guide shirt. It occurs to me that the kid's job is at least partially dependent on catching fish.

The kid recites his résumé to Donicio. Lifetime angler, hunter, lots of guiding experience in Alaska.

"How many trips a year do you do?" Donicio quizzes. "Yeah, like what rivers? What areas?"

Someone suggests that we go and do a little fishing. Me, probably. We get back in the trucks and go.

Another thing I admire about Donicio is that he always looks great in fish pics. It's a skill of his, maybe a guide thing. Not everyone has it. My friend Russ Beck does not, for instance. His hands look like the shaved paws of a bear, and after years of fly-fishing, he's never quite figured out how to hold up a fish without occluding almost its entire body.

I can be counted on to properly pose the fish, but I myself always look uncomfortable in photos—I become too aware of the photo-taking, and my face takes on a pinched, camera-conscious scowl.

Donicio's fish pics are notable because the camera always manages to capture him in a moment of hilarious joy, as if just an instant earlier he'd been given the best news of his life, which also happened to be the funniest thing he'd ever heard. Not that I've taken many fish pics of Donicio. That's another unfortunate reality of my fishing experiences with him—we never seem to hit the jackpot he's always chasing. Our trips are often on the low-volume side, fish-wise.

We once fished the Henry's Fork with our mutual friend Ken, the laconic Colorado Baptist. The fishing was poor. At lunchtime, the only thing we had to talk about was how conspicuously fishless the morning had been, despite Donicio's continuous forecasts to the contrary. As we finished eating and made ready to shove the drift boat back into the current, Ken registered his discontent by pitching the landing net onto the grassy bank and exclaiming, "Welp, won't be needing *this*!"

I don't know if the fishing will be any better at Willard Bay, but I've got a backup plan in case it's worse.

Donicio parks along a swampy, packed-mud road near the north dike, which is constructed of cyclopean boulders of a uniform size and coarseness, which gives the overall impression of a medieval fortification. The kid pulls up behind us. After we suit up, we hike uphill to the dike, climb up the dry side and then boulder-hop down to the water. The shoreline is higher than the surrounding terrain—the water is pumped up and into Willard Bay.

The dike is strewn with beer cans and bottles, some recently discarded, others so old their labels are weathered clean away. The wind blows in our faces and we cast back at it—valiantly, it seems to me—for thirty-five minutes. After that we give up. There are no spawning shad or rolling wipers. It's too early in the season.

"We'll have to come back," says Donicio, scanning the water and rubbing his chin. "Give it a week or so. I'm telling you. When they're rolling. Bam, bam, bam."

Willard Bay is not where the Bear River empties into the Great Salt Lake, as many believe. Instead, the bay is where the Weber River terminates, the final reservoir of the Weber Basin Project, which furnishes irrigation and culinary water to Utah's increasingly urbanized Wasatch Front.

The Bear River enters the Great Salt Lake four or five miles away. After we give up on the wipers and scrabble back to the top of the dike, I can see it—the mouth of the Bear out in the brackish wastes to the northwest. We walk back down into the marshy outskirts of the bay, which are beginning to darken beneath the shadows of the Promontory Mountains as the sun comes low.

"You guys want to try that?" Donicio asks, pointing his rod at a nearby inlet canal.

The kid's already heading that way. The canal is eighty feet wide, and the slow water looks like lightly creamed coffee. It could hold panfish or brown trout or carp—probably all of these.

The kid's at the bank now, casting diligently, but he doesn't catch anything, and I'm beginning to feel sure that he won't. I unsling my backpack and set it on the ground. I reach inside, bring out my backup plan and uncork it. After a quick nip, I hand it to Donicio, who takes a double slug and then offers it to the kid.

The kid shakes his head and keeps casting. Still no fish.

Donicio takes another slug.

We spread out along the bank. The current is so slow that it's basically still water. I'm reluctant to cast at all because I might luck into the fish the kid needs to get this job. The wind has died, and the setting sun's blazing reflection wobbles on the flat water. A few carp breach like little humpback whales, but none will take a fly. There'll be no fish tonight for any of us. You can kind of feel it.

Donicio emerges the early leader with regard to the backup plan. I give him full custody of the bottle so that I'll be in shape to drive us home. At this point, he's just regaling the kid with his war stories, anyhow. Guiding trips gone wrong, assholic clients, trips gone right, enormous tips, enormous tips despite gone-wrong trips. And he's acting like the kid's already got the job. His urgency to catch fish devolves from job-dependent to something more like "I mean, as long as we're out here fishing it'd be nice to hook something."

Good for the kid.

"You're always looking for a certain *kind* of client," Donicio counsels, his face flushed but grave. "The kind that will always call you first to set up epic trips for them."

The kid nods, casts.

"Never promise fish, though," Donicio cautions, gesturing broadly at Willard Bay, as though it's the only rationale needed to adopt such a policy. "I never make promises, but my clients know I'll do everything I can to put 'em on fish."

The kid's just casting on principle here, trying to hit the canal's far bank with his fly. He almost gets it there.

I set my rod aside and sit in the grass, watching the sun plunge into the stormy sky over the Promontorys. The far-off margins of the Great Salt

Lake ecosystem lie ruddy in the dusk. The braids and channels of the Bear appear to flow out from the sunset itself, glowing like rivers of molten bronze.

Donicio is not disappointed about missing the wipers—like, not in the slightest. The bottle was likely of some service to that end, but this is perhaps what I admire most about the guy: the way he deals with fishing's inevitable disappointments. We rolled the dice, came up snake eyes and Donicio contented himself by simply refusing to acknowledge that it happened. He's a seasoned gambler who is always ready for a lucky streak but never curses the game when it busts him.

We return to the vehicles in gathering darkness. I drive Donicio's 4-Runner, and the kid follows us down I-15 to Ogden to get some burgers. Donicio reclines in the passenger seat with a sort of regal drunkenness, his face beaming and eyes twinkling. Judging by his jovial disposition, you'd think we'd just slayed a passel of wipers. You'd think it was lights out at Willard Bay.

Having killed off the better part of a fifth of 80-proof backup plan, Donicio naturally begins reminiscing about Costa Rica. He says the first time he went, instead of a bottled-water, all-inclusive, Gringo-resort-type trip, he wanted a, you know, like, *authentic* Costa Rican experience, so rather than hiring a guide with any kind of, you know, like, *credentials*, he retained the services of a one-legged gypsy-cab driver named Miguel, who operated the pedals of his seriously vintage Mazda with the same crutch he used in, like, basic freaking *walking*, and who, as it turns out, was also responsible for distributing, like, *scandalous* quantities of high-test cocaine throughout the Republic of Costa Rica, a responsibility he fulfilled even with unwitting passengers aboard (for example, Donicio). So, this practically, like, *antediluvian* Mazda gypsy-cab ended up in districts of Costa Rica that boasted such high levels of authenticity Donicio began to worry for his basic personal freaking bodily *safety*.

"Duuude," says Donicio, elongating the word to its breaking point, "I seriously thought they were gonna freakin' waste my American ass because we're driving all over the freakin' shady areas of San Jose, Costa Rica, in this shit-Mazda-beater with freakin' shopping bags of money and blow in the backseat, and I'm seeing freakin' straight-up drug deals going down right in front of me but so then we end up at this like casino-freaking-strip-joint-club-place, and Miguel introduces me to his cousin, and he's all, 'You come with *me* now,' and I'm like, 'Oookay seriously are you guys gonna waste me now or what? Because I'm like a witness? Is that it? I can keep my freakin' mouth shut!' but Miguel's cousin's all, 'No, no, no, you're my guest, and nothing's going to happen to you!' And so, he takes me in the casino, and it's like dude champagne and gambling and friggin' no spending limit all. Night. Long."

10.

THE GAMBLERS OF LA TIENDA

In the rural village of Franklin, Idaho, population six hundred and change, there is a fuel station and C-store called La Tienda. "The Store," in case your Spanish is rusty.

For boaters and campers looking for sacks of ice or a couple pounds of beef jerky before departing to one of the numerous nearby recreation areas of the Bear River watershed, The Store is the stopover of choice. And, like a lot of little stopovers out here in the West, it's also a lot more than that.

For instance, La Tienda employs around forty people, all but a few of whom live in Franklin, meaning this establishment cuts a paycheck to about one in four of the town's working-age population. La Tienda is also the region's principal supplier of lottery tickets, a very important commodity in Idaho. Furthermore, because it's situated a mere five thousand feet from Idaho's border with Utah, where all gambling is illegal, The Store is famously known as "Home of the Utah Lottery." On the eve of big Powerball jackpots, Mormons embark on a pioneer trek, northward this time instead of westward, into Idaho instead of Zion.

Utahans once relied on La Tienda for another provision widely considered essential: beer. The Store boasts a spacious walk-in refrigerator generously stocked with high-point beer, which, until very recently, was not allowed in Utah supermarkets. Until then, Highway 91 between La Tienda and the Utah state line was one of America's last great bootlegging routes.

Most significantly, every summer holiday weekend, La Tienda's parking lot becomes the beachhead for a massive invasion of recreationists. Enormous

La Tienda, Franklin, Idaho.

pickup trucks hauling boats and ATV trailers jockey up to the gas pumps. RVs loom over the shimmering asphalt like aircraft carriers. Bikers in black leather descend in squadrons of ten and twenty.

Inside, a tin bell is rigged up over the entrance, and the discordant jangle is practically continuous all summer. The queue to the check stands winds through the aisles and back to the beverage coolers. A tanned guy in a country music concert T-shirt with cutoff sleeves waits in line, a case of Miller High Life in each fist and a third on the floor, which he nudges along with his boot. Behind him, a sunburned Harley rider is buying cigarettes and energy drinks, his wraparound shades tilted up onto his forehead to reveal a raccoon mask of pale skin. Over by the candy, a mom in a pink camouflage hoodie scolds her kid: "You can get one thing, Rylee. One! That's *two* things. I said *one*!"

Half the customers are buying two-dollar lottery scratch tickets. Old folks in Sunday duds, young folks with tattoos and Kool-Aid-colored coiffures and entire multigenerational families of migrant workers—all line up to buy stacks of twenty, thirty and fifty tickets. The cashiers don't bat an eye, even when asked for one hundred. Then the gamblers loiter in the aisles and scrape away the gray, rubbery film to reveal their fates.

The tickets have names like Epic Fortune and Make Me Rich. They advertise payouts between $10,000 and $250,000, and the Powerball jackpot might inflate to half a billion, but most winning tickets pay $5 or $10.

The *real* players use winnings of less than $50 to buy more scratchers. They're looking for the serious win, and they remain at the check stands for five minutes to cash out and double down for as long as their luck holds. I once saw a guy win $350 and spend it all on more chances. The cashiers allow this, despite the way it slows the line to a glacial procession—it forks or doubles back on itself, giving rise to low-intensity conflicts about who's ahead of whom.

And so, La Tienda is a sort of pageant of the human experience in which young, old, poor and rich shuffle together through the congested convenience store of life. Some are searching for escape. Many seek epic fortune. Others just want a sack of beef jerky.

But that's not how it is on a cool, blustery Sunday morning in April. With Memorial Day still weeks away, I pull off Highway 91 at La Tienda to find the parking lot basically vacant. I take the spot nearest the entrance.

Evidina works a La Tienda check stand just about every Sunday. She's in her early sixties or thereabout, with a short, poufy hairdo and a permanent deferential smile. Roberta's working, too—she's a few years younger than Evidina, and she wears her blond hair long. She's also a bit flirty. The two ladies lean against the counters, chatting and laughing together in the almost empty store. They don't know my name, but they know I'm a Sunday semi-regular. As I walk in, they add their greetings to the dissonant dinging of the little tin bell over the door.

I collect my usual order: twenty ounces of icy Coke, a package of little chocolate donuts and an Idaho six-pack of high-point apple ale.

Roberta waves me over and says, "I can help ya right here, hon."

We begin our ritual.

"Off to fish again, are ya?"

"Yeah."

"Well, ya've got a nice day for it." (If the weather was bad, she'd say, "Well, looks nasty out there, hon. Stay dry.")

How many times have we done this over the years? Fifty? One hundred?

I ask her, "Could I get a four-piece chicken fingers?"

"Sure thing."

La Tienda's chicken fingers are just breaded strips of breast meat, but they're deep fried in small batches, so they're hot and fresh all day, and they've won modest acclaim among regional connoisseurs of gas station cuisine. Surely, Roberta knew I'd order some, but maybe she feels weird serving them before I ask? My saliva glands pucker as she opens the hot-food cabinet and drops six chicken fingers into a paper sack for me.

"They're a little on the small side today," she says in a conspiratorial murmur, "so I threw in a couple extra for ya." (She does this literally every single time.)

I thank her and she gives me a wink as I turn to go.

It's chilly outside, having rained on and off all morning, but as I climb into my truck, the storm clouds are coasting eastward, and the blue-sky gaps harbor promises of a hot afternoon. With The Store in my rearview mirror, I head for Cub River Canyon.

Mormon prophet Brigham Young named the Cub River, presumably because it's a tributary to the Bear. The Cub River watershed drains thirty-two square miles of rugged Idaho mountain range. The headwaters and the first six miles of the river's approximately twenty-mile total extent are on federal land, so the upper Cub is easily accessible, largely undeveloped and boasts spectacular small-stream fly-fishing.

On the drive up the canyon, I eat half the chicken fingers and set the others aside. My truck rattles up the packed-earth road over washboards and through ponds of mud left by spring snowmelt. The aspen trees are leafing out, their gray and green leaves shimmer in the breeze like sequins.

I pull over at a place that overlooks Willow Flat—a wide marshy valley where the Cub slows and splits into braids that snake through a great marsh of willow. In the chancy sunshine, the channels glimmer like rivulets of fugitive mercury.

On Memorial Day weekend, and every weekend afterward until September, Willow Flat and the surrounding hills will be overrun by armies of ATVs and two-stroke dirt bikes. Dust will coat the roadside foliage like a chalky frost. Every camping spot will be crammed with fifty-foot RV trailers, dogs, thrumming electric generators and dusty kids. Worm anglers will unfold their camp chairs and sit in the actual river channel to fish worms and drink beer.

Today, however, the hilltops are still gleaming white, and reefs of grainy snow linger on the shaded aspects of the canyon. Today, the campground is still closed, barred against vehicles by big steel gates.

Today, the place is mine.

I jump down from my truck and listen. There is only the pink noise of the aspens in the wind—no ATVs or dogs. If Memorial Day at La Tienda is the allegorical tableau of humanity's great and sluggish tides, then this pre-runoff April Sunday on the Cub River is an exposition on fly-fishing in which the performer and audience are all the same person. Every fish caught here today will be caught by me. All of the dialogue will be with myself.

I follow a cow trail downriver. Cub River Canyon is located in the Cache National Forest, the official motto of which is "Land of Many Uses," and in addition to recreational use, much of Cub River Canyon is leased to ranchers for cattle grazing. But the cows aren't here yet, either. The barbed-wire cow fences are still lying on the ground. I step over them gingerly, uneager to snag my waders.

I come to the brow of a hill above a stretch of river where there are three nice beaver ponds and a riffle I want to fish before working up through the flats. A chilly breeze sweeps through as I take an overview.

The place has an unfinished look, as if still preparing for the recreational onslaught to come. Spring runoff has not commenced, but the slightly elevated flow and the milky tint are the river's statements of intent. The riverbanks are muddy, and the willows are mostly bare, like the skeletal framing and scaffolds of in-progress bankside development projects. The hillsides are lush with new growth of mulesear and chokecherry, but there are no blooms. The swallows haven't returned yet, either, but the yellow-headed blackbirds have, and they fill the air with hoarse buzzing calls that remind me of construction noises.

I spot fish darting around in the beaver ponds, and I see a couple rise-rings. As is typical at the Cub, there are a few different insects coming off the water. There aren't enough of any one kind to call it a hatch, but that just means the fish will probably strike at anything today.

All three of the ponds are ramshackle and leaky, perhaps abandoned by their engineers. They're not very wide or deep. In the thalweg of each pond is a little pod of trout. They're moving, chasing, feeding, and every few minutes, one of them surfaces to take the odd snowfly or midge.

I'll start at the lowest pond, fish all three, work up through the riffle and then fish the flats beyond. I leave one bottle of La Tienda apple ale in the water at the bank and wade out into the tail of the lowermost beaver pond. My waders compress in the hip-deep water, and I feel its chilly grip through my Levis.

At the outfall, I plant myself like a lottery player at La Tienda and start scratching tickets, hoping for a winner.

In this part of the river, there are lots of brook trout, vividly gilded, pernicious little descendants of nonnative fish that were indiscriminately stocked all over the West in the early 1900s. There are rainbow trout here, too, but these were stocked just last spring by the Idaho Fish and Game Department. These stockies are genetically sterile put-and-take fish meant for anglers who want to keep and kill their catch. The rainbows remaining here now are those that have managed to evade capture for a season or two. They were pale and small when they arrived—no more than ten inches. After a year or more in the fecund, marshy maze of the flats, they've colored up and grown to twelve or fourteen inches. Multi-season holdovers can go eighteen inches. Nice fish. Fun to catch. But I'm not terribly interested in palm-sized invasives from back east, nor blunt-nose put-and-take fish native only to concrete raceways. I'm a regular here, looking for the serious win. I'm looking for cutthroats.

The Bonneville cutthroat trout is the only trout native to the Bear River watershed. They've been squeezed and abused by agriculture, water development and nonnative species introductions, but a remnant of them has, against narrow odds, survived here, and it is this Ur-trout I'm most interested in.

Lucky for me, the cutthroats are on the move, swimming upriver to their spawning grounds. Right now, the water is still too low, slow and

Willow Flat Bonneville cutthroat trout.

clear for them to build redds, but they're arriving, quietly speculating on prime real estate and staking out territory before spring runoff. That's my theory, anyway.

I cast a Stimulator to the top of the beaver pond and let it glide down the center. The most foolhardy trout in the pond rises—an overwintered rainbow stockie. I set the hook and horse him hastily back to me at the tailout so he won't spook the others. After unhooking him, I turn him around and launch him downstream. I cast the same way again and catch the second-most foolhardy fish, another rainbow. After that, they don't rise to the Stimulator, so I tie on a nymph dropper with iridescent wingcase and peacock herl thorax. With this I hook a couple more fish—those too lazy to come all the way to the top but hungry enough to break ranks and hit a fly at mid-column. Lastly, I trail a heavily weighted caddis nymph beneath an indicator on four feet of 4X tippet, trying to dredge the bottom and round up that final fish who insists on having the fly steered practically right into his mouth.

I run this play at the second pond and then the third, and the results are comparable—three or four trout from each pond. But they're all brook trout and rainbow stockies. No cutts.

I move upstream and see the riffle. It's thirty feet wide and runs no more than three feet deep between sloped, grassy banks, describing a very elongated *S* about 150 yards long. The substrate consists of cobbles interspersed with boulders the size of prize-winning pumpkins.

It's obvious now why I caught only brookies and rainbows downstream—cutthroats staging up for runoff and the ensuing sex bonanza aren't interested in deep, silt-bottomed beaver ponds. Instead, they'll be here in the shallow, gravelly sections where the spawning will actually occur. That's what I tell myself, anyway.

I cast the Stimulator to a few of the cobbles and boulders, first to the slipstream behind and then to the pillow of current in front. I catch a couple really nice rainbows. I hook a brookie just an inch longer than my index finger. But still no cutthroats.

The thing is, I've caught the pre-spawn cutthroats here before. Twelve-inchers, fourteen-inchers and larger. Sleek, determined-looking trout, their speckled backs are a burnt shade of gold, and their cheek plates and chin slashes are fluorescent fuchsia. I've come up Highway 91 many times in March and April to wait in line behind the gamblers of La Tienda with my high-point apple ale and little chocolate donuts. I've made mannerly, weather-related patter with Roberta five dozen times. She's probably comped me $100 worth of supplemental under-sized chicken fingers. One day, after observing all of these rituals, I proceeded up into the early spring lushness of Cub River Canyon to hook a pre-spawn Bear River cutthroat trout that was eighteen inches long. As I lifted him from the net, he felt heavy, not just with muscle but with the legacy and potential of his own embattled species.

I've come not to test my hypothesis but to validate it—I've caught the cutts here before at this time of year more times that I can count. Just not today, apparently.

At the bottom of the canyon, the Cub flows out of the Cache National Forest and leaks unceremoniously into the pasturelands of southeastern Idaho, where it runs over grim muddy bottoms and between shadeless, eroded banks. Down there, the Cub more closely resembles a canal of watery chocolate milk than a freestone river. Some sections are desiccated by irrigation claims. The river eventually skulks across the state line and empties into an algae-smothered section of the Bear out back of an old granary in Richmond, Utah. You wouldn't want to fish there even if it wasn't on private land. This is common in the Bear River watershed—tributaries of crystalline trout-friendly waters rising on public land that then flow onto private property and devolve into warm, lifeless ditches.

Up here in the Cache National Forest, however, in the cold fast flow of the upper Cub, in this pre-ATV nirvana, I should be content to have a stretch of river to myself for the day. No fly angler has any right to ask for more than a day of solitude and a fish hooked cleanly in the lip. But I double down and cast to each and any favorable spot. I cast up under the banks, change flies and add a dropper, scratching furiously at each ticket.

And I catch a break.

A cutthroat that'd been hanging out down in a little scour behind a boulder just off the bank darts up to eat my plain old Elk Hair Caddis. I almost miss him, and I worry that he's not hooked well.

But he stays on, hooked cleanly in the bone of his lip. I keep him in the water. He lies on his side in my net and stares up at me. At just twelve inches, this cutthroat is no epic fortune, but he is a winner. The fly comes out without any coaxing. Then the fish is gone.

For a while, I sit on the riverbank with my boots in the water. It's gotten warm, and the wind has quit the valley. All at once it feels like summer. The yellow-headed blackbirds bicker the afternoon away. Willow Flat spreads quietly before me like a boundless open book.

Then a fly angler appears upstream—a young guy. He hasn't seen me, and he's quick-stepping down the bank like maybe he's trying to beat someone to the water's edge. He's approximately ten seconds away from high-holing me. I guess I was wrong. Someone else has gotten in line; another actor has taken the stage.

"Hey," I call out.

He stops. "Oh. Hey. Didn't see you. Didn't think anyone was down here. That your truck up above?"

So, not a very *good* actor.

"Yeah," I answer.

He points upstream with his flyrod at the unspoiled flats. "So, you fishing up through here?"

That's actually a good question.

I remember the bottle of ale I stashed in the first beaver pond and the spare chicken strips wrapped in the paper sack translucent with fry oil. I think about the cutthroat, framed in the water by the bow of my net, flaring his gills and looking up at me with an expression that seemed to ask, "Happy now?"

Yeah, I suppose I am.

"No," I tell the young intruder. "I just finished up. It's all yours."

II.

CONSIDER THE MAYFLY

The sun beamed down through a partly cloudy sky, glistering on the Blacksmith Fork like jewels that had floated to the surface. It was warm but not hot. There was no wind. Best of all, the mayflies were hatching massively, those partly clouds keeping them on the water for long downstream voyages, and the trout rose to devour them.

Sometimes the fish showed just their noses, and sometimes they jumped clear of the water. Swallows swooped in to feast, too, often picking off two airborne mayflies before veering away. In the still, warm air, the mayflies did not so much take flight as fall as though by reverse gravity.

Could there be a better day to fish a freestone stream? To cast dry flies? No and also no.

So, you'd think any half-suitable presentation of any half-decent fly would result in a hooked trout half the time. And yet I stood there in the water with a flyrod, my cast petulant and sloppy. Because despite the jumping fish and sublime sunlight, I'd been fishing for an hour without catching anything. It's fairly common for my technique to suffer when the fishing is poor, but this is especially true when the other guy is catching fish without appearing to try very hard.

Russ knelt in the stream on the right bank and released another brown trout as I recovered another fumbled cast on the left.

"Sorry," said Russ, cringing. He stood and flicked the water from his hand. "Wanna switch sides again?"

"Nah," I said, waving him onward. "Let's keep going."

Hatching mayflies. *Courtesy of Tyler Coleman.*

I'd waited five months for this, fishing through winter, catching just a few fish per outing sometimes, desperate and yet reluctant trout, often small. I'd fished through the turbulent pre-spring—one day it was warm and windless when I got out of the truck and then blowing sideways snow when I'd gotten my waders on.

Now I'd made it to May. I was due.

The fish were biting, that much was clear; they just weren't biting on my side of the stream, regardless of which side that happened to be. Russ set his hook on another brown. In this middle section of the Blacksmith Fork, there was a population of Bonneville cutthroats, but brown trout predominated.

"Sorry," repeated Russ, playing the trout into his net. "Oooh, he's a nice one, though. Check him out."

"Yeah," I said without looking, "nice one."

I pulled out my flybox to switch flies, but the fly wasn't to blame. Something else was off. I couldn't get into the zone, couldn't find my flow—whatever terms they were currently using to describe that state of mindful blankness or hazy mindfulness. And the day was slipping away fast, like it does when the fishing is good but not good for you. I needed to zen it up soon.

The fly I chose looked slightly different than the one I'd been using but hardly more like the mayfly I was trying to imitate. I glanced up at the declining sun before I clipped off the old fly and tied on the new one. Before I began to cast, I let my gaze follow the mayflies drifting past my legs.

It's widely believed that mayflies live for only one day, but most species of mayfly live for an entire year, and for some species it's two. They stood on the surface of the Blacksmith Fork, their feet pressing tiny, almost imperceptible dimples into the water. Gliding downstream with their wings upright, they resembled a regatta of rudderless catamarans.

As I watched one plump specimen race along just a few feet from where I stood, a brown trout appeared, opened a void in the water and mayfly and trout vanished together.

"I'd really love to know what I gotta do to catch a fish today," I muttered.

"Yeah, I have no clue," Russ replied blithely as his fish swam away. "I usually don't. Change flies maybe?"

I nodded. "That's an idea."

"Ope—'nother fish. Sorry."

I hadn't counted on catching fifty fish or a trophy brown. The Blacksmith Fork seldom offered such opportunities. I didn't even care who caught more

Bear River brown trout.

fish. All I sought was "the usual," a sunny day in the canyon to stand in cool, fast water and maybe net a few nice trout—an afternoon of respite.

Respite from what, you might ask. Certainly nothing too, like, *dire*. Heavy spring rains had flooded my basement. A windstorm had knocked a big limb off the giant Japanese elm in my yard, demolishing a section of rain gutter on my house. There were also concerns of a more general nature—too many hours at work, too little time off, the sense that I'd simply never catch up.

Oh, and there was this other weird thing that kept happening: every now and then I'd be overcome with a panicky awareness of my lifetime piling up behind me with only a short time ahead. Your typical midlife crisis. Would I achieve anything remarkable in the time I had left? Forget remarkable—would I do anything *interesting*? Or was I just another insect skating weightlessly over a thin membrane of peril, waiting for a void to open ignominiously beneath me?

We slogged upstream into the Dogleg, where the river backed up in a pair of opposing bend pools known to hold trout. I made a few casts with my new fly, and, to my mild surprise, I hooked a very small brown trout.

"Hey, hey!" gushed Russ. "Ya got one." I think he wanted to add "finally," but he refrained.

"Just a shrimpy one," I complained, releasing the fish without fanfare.

The curse had lifted, kind of, but the trout barely put a bend in my flyrod. After a few more casts, I caught another much like the first—scarcely longer than my hand and meager consolation considering the burlier browns Russ was bagging.

For a freestone stream with an average annual flow of only about 150 cubic feet per second, the Blacksmith Fork is nevertheless a hatch chaser's dream. Prolific mayfly hatches might start strong in April, continue throughout summer and persist into autumn's hard freezes.

Likewise, caddisfly hatches begin tentatively in June and grow increasingly conspicuous until September, often spilling into October. You can count on little black stoneflies and midge hatches from January to late April, and I've been told there's a really good cranefly hatch in the fall.

Green drakes emerge in successive waves up and down the Blacksmith Fork in early June. On the Left Hand Fork, a tight brushy tributary of the Blacksmith, green drake hatches are profuse on certain days. For several weeks, Green Wulffs, Adams, Comparaduns and similar big patterns are productive in the entire drainage, even when drakes aren't hatching.

The Blacksmith Fork even harbors the giant salmonfly (*Pteronarcys californica*), which hatch for two or three weeks between mid-April and late June.

Caddisflies, stoneflies and salmonflies contribute much more than mayflies to the nourishment of Blacksmith Fork trout, but I will always think of this river first as mayfly water. Memories of catching dozens of shoaled-up browns on nearly invisible upwing dries during blizzard-hatch conditions are some of the fondest I have from my early days of fly-fishing.

No such memories were catalogued that day at the Dogleg. The brown trout rose, swallows swooped and the mayflies floating up were lit by the lowering sun like swarms of candlelight free of their wicks. The hatch strengthened as the day lengthened. Mayflies landed on our hats and shirtsleeves. Still, I did the fishing while Russ did the catching.

One reason for the misconception about mayflies is that the final and most critical phase of their life cycle lasts just one day. The mayfly begins life as an egg so tiny it's nearly invisible to the naked eye. Slightly denser than water, the egg sinks to the riverbed. A couple weeks later, a mayfly nymph hatches and burrows into the sand and sediment. Speckled and primitive looking, the nymph simultaneously resembles a crab, shrimp and trilobite. It lives on the undersides of rocks, eats algae, hides from trout and awaits its first and only birthday. When that day arrives, it's as if, after a lifetime of staying home, the mayfly larvae collectively decide it's time to get off their asses, see the world and find love. So, they swim up together from the blackness.

And the fish are waiting for them.

Mayflies have no defenses, and trout eat many of them before they ever get close to emerging. It's only by virtue of the mayflies' synchronous plentitude that some fraction of them survive the passage from water to air. The more prolific and precisely timed the hatch, the greater their reproductive success, but the clock is ticking—they have just hours to live.

Mayfly larva are so small and feeble that the water's surface is like a tough, rubbery film they must pierce and wriggle through. Many don't make it, and we fly anglers rather insensitively call them cripples. They smother in the surface film, and the fish feed on them there too.

The larvae that reach the air and shuffle off their nymphal shucks are promoted to sub-imagos, or what anglers call duns. It's difficult to overstate how fragile and hapless the duns are. Frail and clumsy, they are immediately attacked from every direction. The smallest trout ascends like a leviathan from the murk below, and the swallows thunder down like fighter jets from above. The insects have no means to evade the rising fish and no way to steer in flight. Strong breezes and rough water can be catastrophic. Their only hope is that water currents steer them clear of hungry trout and air currents waft them away from hungry birds. Luck is their sole ally.

As it is with many insects, mayflies require ultraviolet light to stiffen their newly deployed wings and skin before they can do anything. This might be why fish rise better to mayflies on overcast days—with less direct sunlight, the process takes longer. The same is true when it rains—the meteoric raindrops inflict more casualties.

But if a dun can escape the river and hole up somewhere for just a few hours, its skin will split open and a better, stronger version of itself will emerge. More agile in flight, they're called imagos, but we call them spinners. As the sun sets, these survivors return to the river, find a partner and mate in midair.

Only after they've dispersed the seeds of a new generation into the stream do the mayflies at last lay their wings on the water in an elegant suicide ritual. Here the fish feed on them one last time, throughout the evening and sometimes into the next day.

Although they are mere insects without human traits, I imagine a certain satisfaction in their ending—the mayfly sails through a gauntlet of disasters with nothing more than chance as an ally, achieving its objective or dying in the attempt.

Russ and I got out of the river at the pumphouse and walked back to the truck as the sun slid behind the western wall of the canyon.

"Well," said Russ, shuffling off his waders, "that was awesome."

"When we consider the mayfly, we consider ourselves." *Courtesy of Kyle Jensen.*

As I stowed my gear, I considered the mayflies and felt suddenly content. My basement was still damp. The crumpled rain gutter waited. And even reckoning optimistically, I'd come halfway through the years I'd likely be allotted, and I could do little about the way my remaining time seemed to blur past faster as I got older, which meant that even if I had fully half my life ahead of me, it would feel like much less.

Nevertheless, there at the tailgate of my truck, I was struck by a wave of irrational equanimity. In the yawning immensity of cosmic time, a lifespan of seventy or eighty earth years is no different than the final day of a mayfly. I could live to 150 and it'd still feel like an eyeblink.

"Yeah," I confessed. "I guess it was pretty all right."

We all hurtle downstream over rough waves, beset from every side, and even those with few hardships exist for only an instant. So, there is little profit in complaining, dwelling on future catastrophes or contemplating our own clumsiness. When we consider the mayfly, we consider ourselves. The best thing you can do—the only thing you can do—is become the strongest and boldest version of yourself, find a purpose and chase it as if each day is your last.

12.

BLACK CANYON SLACKER BACHELORS

Too much fishing wasn't the reason I got divorced. Unlike many other anglers, I demolished my marriage without bringing trout into it at all. This is not to say I didn't fish more after the divorce. I certainly did. Even during the separation, I was fishing two or three times a week, which goes to show that sometimes the only way to have more time on the water is to get the courts involved.

In their attempts to avoid making me feel awkward, my married fishing buddies made me feel so awkward that I had to quit fishing with anyone whose marriage was even marginally successful. So, I fished instead with my friend Jason Reed, a shaggy-bearded neo-hippie bachelor introvert who possessed two important attributes: first, a sardonic baritone laugh and second, a pathological aversion to broaching the topic of marital strife.

As with many great friendships, Jason and mine began when one of us inadvertently became the unpaid employee of the other. Jason was still in college back then, finishing a natural resources degree, and he'd enrolled in one of those upper-division classes that, instead of lectures and exams, required time-sucking practicums and jumping through pointless real-world hoops, presumably to show students what life was like after graduation.

One such hoop was to volunteer for a nonprofit organization, and Jason chose the local chapter of Trout Unlimited, of which I was president. He probably figured he'd earn college credit for fly-fishing, but Jason's professor told me that I could order Jason to wax my truck as long as I left the final

Bear River at Black Canyon.

impression that nonprofit work is often thankless and almost always futile. I assured the professor that wouldn't be a problem.

Jason's first assignment was to comb through our chapter's outdated membership spreadsheet and contact any members who hadn't been attending our meetings. Many of them had probably quit the chapter, some had maybe moved away, certainly some had *passed* away and a few might have accomplished all three. I needed someone to call these codgers, enquire whether they were alive or dead and invite the still-living back to the chapter.

Jason wasn't thrilled about this. After a week, I asked him, "How's that membership list coming?"

"Well, I've called a few of these old dudes," he reported, "but they're all super grouchy and suspicious, and they don't really seem like they wanna be contacted."

I pointed out that this was essentially the definition of "fly angler." However, I didn't have the heart to make him finish the project. We went fishing instead. So, Jason really did get college credit for fly-fishing, because although the membership list was still in tatters, I told the professor that Jason should receive full marks for his efforts.

Jason and I fished even more after my divorce. We'd meet on Sunday morning in the parking lot of a decommissioned Kmart and go fish the Cub River all day. On Tuesday afternoon, we'd maybe hit Curtis Creek and fish until dark. On Wednesday, I'd ditch work and fish the Logan. Then on Saturday morning, I'd meet Jason again, and we'd head to Rock Creek or back to the Cub. After each trip, we'd lean against our trucks in the ghostly Kmart parking lot, watching the sunset and talking about fish or kung fu movies or Jethro Tull records.

When it was dark, we'd decide where and when to fish next. "So, whaddya think, Leroy?" (Jason was and still is one of the few people who calls me by my middle name.) "Spring Hollow in the morning? Meet at nine? Okay. See you then."

It never took much longer than that, because I was no longer legally obligated to the woman in my life, and Jason didn't have one in his. I admired his sardonic bachelor refrain: "I've got a truck and a dog. What do I need a woman for?"

Soon I was a slacker bachelor myself and fishing so much that my laundry and dirty dishes stood in great heaps around my dim basement bachelor pad. Some weeks I'd go fishing every single day, just because I could. It was probably the closest I'll ever come to being a trout bum.

When I wasn't fishing, I drunk binge-watched *Breaking Bad* and dallied with an attractive brunette paramour whose temperament fell somewhere between Holly Golightly on a bad day and Scarlet O'Hara on a good one.

Jason faced his own challenges, which aren't mine to talk about, so I won't say whether he had girl troubles or work drama or some other species of bullshit. As we drove to the river, I'd ask him, "So, how's things?"

"Oh, getting a little better, I guess," he'd reply. "Or a lot worse. Fuck if I know." Then he'd laugh his dark baritone laugh.

The Black Canyon section of the Bear River became our preferred spot to fish. It's near Grace, Idaho, and it took us almost an hour and a half to drive there. Some would say that's too far for one day of fishing, while others might think it's not far enough to really get away. That section of the river is known for dramatic midge and blue-wing olive hatches. On one trip there with my fishing buddies Russ and Brad, I waded out to cover a promising mid-channel slick and from that one spot caught nineteen trout in one hour.

But Black Canyon is notoriously mercurial. You fish there the same way you act around a girl you suspect is getting bored with you—play it cool, keep expectations low and if she dumps you, shrug it off by saying you saw it coming.

The canyon is named for the basaltic rock formations so common in that part of Idaho. The river channel is 150 feet across, its banks buttressed by black boulders as big as fridges. Rather than a pool-riffle-glide form, the Bear cuts through Black Canyon via a series of terraced pools, like water flooding down a gentle staircase. The water flows from one terrace into the next over falls a few feet high. The bottom is travertine, a porous, low-density form of accreted limestone that is cratered like swiss cheese so that each terrace encompasses a honeycomb of bowls and basins.

To fish Black Canyon, we didn't tread up the middle of the river. It was too deep and wide and irregular for that. Rather, we stepped crabwise across the downstream lip of one terrace pool, prospecting its recesses, most of which were too deep to see the bottom. Then we'd move upstream and wade crossways along the lower lip of the next pool.

I think we settled on Black Canyon not in spite of the long distance and iffy odds but because of them. We wanted the ninety-minute drive, regardless of the fish.

"Well, dude," Jason would say, "should we go back to Black and see how many fish we don't catch?"

As a place to ruminate about life, Black Canyon was ideal. If pondering my recent choices was what I wanted to do, I was seldom distracted by too many fish. And if I wanted to do anything *but* ponder my choices, numberless waterfalls generated a ceaseless, mind-clearing pink noise that made the real world seem a lot farther away than ninety minutes.

Black Canyon was also metaphorically situated for someone who'd made such dramatic course changes. Because if you run your finger along the Bear River on a map, trace it northwestward from the Uintas, you'll soon come to Soda Point in Idaho, where the river breaks unexpectedly left.

Black Canyon is where the Bear River goes south.

It didn't always take that turn. The Bear River's prehistoric course continued northwest, flowing past Grace to the Portneuf River, which eventually empties into the Columbia River drainage before proceeding nobly to the Pacific Ocean. About 140,000 years ago, however, cataclysmic volcanic eruptions near Soda Point blocked the river and diverted it southward. This new course helped create Lake Bonneville, an ancient pluvial waterbody that covered half of Utah with one thousand feet of water. But it also contributed to the self-destruction of the lake, which overtopped its banks and breached about 15,000 years ago at Red Rock Pass. Lake Bonneville drained, leaving behind the Great Salt Lake, which still relies on the Bear for most of its inflow. At approximately 1,700 square miles, the Great Salt Lake is vast, but it's a puny remnant of Lake Bonneville, which at peak elevation covered a staggering 20,000 square miles.

As Jason and I drove back and forth to Black Canyon, we were turning out of our own personal banks, overtopping, breaching, not knowing which direction we'd turn next. I went there many times wondering if the divorce was a mistake or wondering not if the volcanic brunette paramour would dump me, but when.

Summer was the worst season at Black Canyon, when all of the water was held back five miles upstream behind Grace Dam for irrigation and hydroelectricity. Flows dropped to accretion from nearby springs. The water temperature rose, and moss blossomed from the travertine, forming great waving mats that covered the mouths of the pools. This not only made the fly-fishing a bummer but also ensured that one wrong step could plunge you neck-deep into a kind of watery tiger trap. We fished with expectations so low that we were practically double-dog daring the river to produce a fish.

Fall and winter were better. The flows remained low, but the moss was gone, and the water was at least cold. Nymphing with long leaders and heavy flies wrapped in neon tinsel paid off with big fish pulled up from their overwintering deeps. There was the occasional profuse midge hatch, but these required very rapid rerigging because sometimes the midges hatched for only ten minutes.

Early spring was best. The flows increased and the fish turned active. Small trout went after dry flies with gusto, and larger specimens might move for streamers or a big buggy Pheasant Tail.

It was springtime midge hatches that gave Jason and me our best days at Black Canyon. One Saturday, we hiked downstream to a broad waterfall with a thundering plunge pool. We'd fished there before without much success. It was very deep and pushy. We could wade out only about ten feet, and to reach the productive mid-channel runs, long, mend-intensive casts were called for. Fishing that day at the big pool was slow, so I sat on a boulder to watch Jason cast into the sun, which hovered just a finger's breadth above the western ridge of the canyon. There were no midges on the water, but Jason tied a microscopic Zebra Midge beneath a strike indicator, and on this Hail Mary hunch, he hooked a fantastic fifteen-inch cutthroat. Then he caught another. I hopped down from my boulder.

The midges were just then beginning to lift off the water. They twinkled in the slanted light. Fish were leaving little tattle-tale boils at the surface as they fed on the emergers, but these were tough to spot in the effervescent upwellings below the waterfall. Jason was casting into the far-off mid-channel runs, and every time he managed a well-mended drift, another cutt would yank his indicator beneath the foaming water.

After fishing midge hatches all winter, I had only a couple of Zebra Midges in my flybox, but as soon as I got one tied on and out into the flow, I caught a few of the big cutties too.

And then the sun dove behind the ridge, a shadow fell across the river and it all shut down.

"It's 4:45," I observed.

"Started about a quarter after, I think," Jason replied.

We fished wishfully for another hour and then reeled in.

"Back here tomorrow, Leroy?"

That night I set up my vise in front of the TV. While Walter White cooked wholesale quantities of blue meth, I tied black Zebra Midges with silver wire bodies and glass-bead heads. By the time I'd finished, Jesse was pursuing his own stormy, dark-haired lover, but we all know how that turned out.

Around lunchtime the next day, we drove back to Black, and at exactly 4:10 p.m., the waterfall midge hatch started up again. The cutts were ready for the midges, and we were ready for the cutts.

I often wonder how long it took the Bear to settle into its new southward course all those millennia ago, how long before it resembled a river and not just a formless brown flood running over previously arid scrub desert. How long for the riverbed, floodplain, aquatic ecology and the Bonneville cutthroats to become established? Ten years? One thousand?

Jason and I returned a few times that spring, checking the big pool for midges, but we never really replicated those two days.

A year after the Black Canyon slacker bachelor excursions, I proposed to the brunette paramour. Within another year, we were married. A year after that, Jason found a girl who evidently superseded the bachelor utility of his dog and truck, and he got engaged too. But I could never guess how long it might take us to settle into our new courses, how long to resemble something more than formless floods in the desert. The canyons we'd stalked and the dark, alienesque bedrock of southeastern Idaho were often surprising, even to us.

13.

LONG JOHN SILVER AND
THE CLACKAMAS CUCKOO

I can't remember exactly who told me, "You oughta check out some a'them little feeder creeks up above Blacksmith Fork." He was a friendly old fellow, but this was years ago, and I don't recall his name anymore or how I met him. I wish I did. It's good to keep a lineage of such things.

Probably, I knew him through Trout Unlimited. Back then I was a chapter president, which put me in touch with lots of old fly anglers who, when forced indoors, often grew eager to announce how much they knew.

The fellow scrawled a crude map. His handwriting was on the sloppy side, by which I mean illegible, but this was the sort of map John Gierach counts as more valuable than any map issued by the Forest Service or USGS—the napkin-back map passed from one angler to another at a bar or, in my case, a fly shop. Two intersecting lines represented State Route 101 and Ant Flat Road, like the *X* on a treasure map, and a wavy line stood for the creek.

He tapped the wavy line. "You can catch some real good fish in there," he said, holding his index fingers about sixteen inches apart. "Thing is, it's real skinny water most'a the time, real brushy, so not a lotta people g'wup there."

Such fishing tips are like those that pour in after the FBI announces a big manhunt—you want to bust the case wide open, but you can't trust every friendly but penmanship challenged and possibly prone to exaggerate chap you meet.

Nevertheless, the prospect of a little creek full of big trout where no one else fished was of some interest to me. You could say I was interested in that sort of thing. So, I shrugged, and one day late in spring, I followed the map into Blacksmith Fork Canyon with the skeptical obligation of a homicide detective following a lead involving black helicopters and mind-control lasers. I parked where the map said to, and there was in fact a creek nearby. The story checked out thus far, so I got on my waders.

A first-order tributary to the Blacksmith Fork, the creek flowed down from high in the drainage. The Division of Wildlife had fenced the lower extent with a tall exclosure to keep out elk and livestock. Inside the fence there sprawled a jungle of willows and reeds and shoulder-high grass, all lousy with western tanagers and cedar waxwings.

At one time, there had evidently been fences and footbridges along the stream, but the channel's unchecked migration had overwhelmed these features, which now lay half-digested and subsiding into the water. Some of the streambanks were so undercut that you could hide a Honda Civic underneath.

The fellow was right about the size. It was the smallest water I'd ever seriously fished. But it wasn't just skinny. It felt miniaturized. The bends were tiny and tight, and the runs were so short that I could cast to the next pool without moving up from the last. It was like looking at a river from an airplane.

To describe the stream as multi-braided would likewise be an understatement. This stream was insanely braided. Beaver dams shunted the water into numerous side channels, some of which were fast and loud, others slow and oxbow-like. They looped around on each other, which made it seem like the water flowed in all directions at once.

But the trout were there.

As the old fellow claimed, brown trout sixteen inches and better were not uncommon, and there were Bonneville cutthroats, too—it was a nursery for the cutts and a feeding ground for the browns.

The fellow was right about one last thing: no one else fished the place. I returned on weekends and weekdays, and I seldom had any company. I figured my fellow anglers assumed the exclosure fencing meant it was off-limits. It was starting to feel like maybe what had happened was that I'd found a little creek full of big trout where no one else fished.

So, I did the only sensible thing: I fished the goddamn hell out of it.

The place required some figuring out. There were sinkholes on the banks and snarls of rotting barbed wire to avoid. Wide-open casting lanes were few, and when my fly wasn't snagged in the grass in my backcast, I was untwisting tippet from willow boughs that drooped smugly into every promising lie. I thought the woolly vegetation would screen me from being seen by fish, but there were secret braids that held fish I didn't even know were looking my way, which likely didn't matter anyhow, because the boggy, peat-like ground telegraphed my footsteps twenty yards upstream and down.

However, one thing I did perfectly was keep my big mouth shut. Unlike the fellow who'd tipped me off, I didn't say a word about the stream to anyone. In fact, I fished it for that entire summer before I bothered to locate it on a map.

Once I mastered the angles, it wasn't hard to catch thirty fish in a few hours. The cutthroats ate just about any downwing pattern I offered, and the chunky, piscivorous browns took dries and streamers both. All this in solitude. Still, every time I fished there, I gave myself away and missed good fish.

This is where Sheridan Anderson's masterpiece *The Curtis Creek Manifesto* enters the tale and the lore of the Bear River watershed itself. For the uninitiated, the *Manifesto*, released in 1978 by Frank Amato Publications of Portland, Oregon, is perhaps the greatest instructional fly-fishing book ever written and one of the most richly storied books in all of fish lit. This might sound like a bit much for what is essentially a forty-eight-page comic book, but the *Manifesto* is so clear, so enlightening that each illustration is literally worth a thousand words. The book is known worldwide and stands without deference beside Isaak Walton's *The Compleat Angler* and all the writings of Leeson, McGuane and Gierach.

As a fly angler, I'm mostly self-taught, and because I lacked aptitude as both instructor and pupil, Anderson's *Manifesto* was instrumental in my initial, fumbling grasp of the basics. Any concept or technique not explained in his book is probably superfluous to catching trout on the fly. The *Manifesto*'s advice is especially relevant for fishing small, technical waterways. So, I fell back on the *Manifesto*'s lessons when visiting my newly discovered creek. The skinny water and spooky fish dared me to cast better, think harder and practice the brute force of patience.

First, I embraced Anderson's prescription of penitential stealth, crawling on hands and knees to the stream and sometimes slithering on my belly like some gargantuan otter. I ruined high-dollar waders kneeling so much in the streambed. "Mustn't scare!" became my credo. For the first time, I caught fish on the slingshot cast, a technique I'd previously considered largely theoretical, not to mention really show-offy. And the Curtis Creek sneak became not just a nifty trick from some funny old book—it was the go-to cast.

But these advancements and the many fish I caught turned out to be mere footnotes to that summer. Something much more poignant happened. In a blindsiding epiphany, that summer I learned Sheridan Anderson had not only penned the book of beautifully bullshit-free advice I needed for fishing that very creek, but Anderson himself had also *fished* that very creek. The stream the *Manifesto* is named for and the stream I was fishing were one and the same.

I don't mean this in some misty, metaphysical way. I mean when I finally found the stream on a topo map, I discovered that the little feeder stream was *the* Curtis Creek.

Back then I didn't know much about Sheridan Anderson. I idolized him as a cartoonist and fly-fishing authority, but I'd never researched his life and times. And I hadn't fished the Bear River watershed enough to know about Curtis Creek. However, I quickly learned that Sheridan Anderson was born in California in 1936, but he was raised in Utah, where he fly-fished the Blacksmith Fork and Curtis Creek.

I spoke about Anderson with Frank Amato. It was over his transom that Anderson proffered the first fifteen xeroxed pages of his *Manifesto* back in the mid-1970s.

"Right away I knew it was something good," Amato told me, "so I flew out to San Francisco. Sheridan picked me up at the airport. First time I saw him, it was like meeting Long John Silver. He was six-two, great big guy. He had this big black felt hat on, just like a pirate. A fly-fishing pirate."

The impression was not unintentional; Anderson often referred to himself as a pirate and even wore a cape at times. He certainly played the role of a nomadic pleasure-seeker and "eternal foe of the work ethic," but his real life was probably less than truly carefree. His younger brother, Mike, once stated that their early family life was darkened by domestic turmoil and alcoholism, problems that followed Sheridan into adulthood.

"He drank heavily," said Amato. "I guess he had his demons. But, you know, who doesn't?"

After dropping out of University of Utah, Anderson moved to California and became a sort of hard-drinking fly-fishing liaison to West Coast counterculture. He fished with Yvon Chouinard and climbed on El Capitan with Royal Robbins out of Camp 4 at Yosemite National Park in the early 1960s. Anderson was an illustrator and cartoonist for several iconic climbing magazines, including the often-raunchy *Vulgarian's Digest* (under the pen name E. Lovejoy Wolfinger III so as not to mortify his more respectable clientele), and he illustrated two instructional climbing books for Robbins.

In the mid-1960s, Anderson lived in post-Beat Haight-Ashbury, crossing paths with many counterculture luminaries, including underground cartoonists Robert Crumb and S. Clay Wilson and gonzo journalists Hunter

Curtis Creek brown trout.

S. Thompson and Warren Hinckle. When Anderson began working on the *Manifesto*, he sought inspiration at the venerable Golden Gate Park casting pools and the Winston fly shop in San Francisco, epicenters of the American fly-fishing scene.

But even after the *Manifesto* was released, Anderson was usually partially employed and partially homeless, likely working harder as an itinerant epicurean than he ever would at a nine-to-five job.

"I had him over for dinner one time," Amato recalled with fondness. "My wife cooked for us. We sat down, and she'd cooked these two big pot roasts. I think she had the idea that we'd eat one for dinner and make sandwiches with the other one later, but pretty soon I looked over and realized Sheridan'd polished off one whole pot roast and part of the other one."

In return, Anderson entertained the couple, flamboyantly demonstrating his stealthy fishing techniques, creeping and casting along Kellogg Creek, which flowed past Amato's home. He even spangled one of Amato's T-shirts with fly-fishing cartoons.

Golden Gate Angling & Casting Club, San Francisco, California.

"So, then I asked Sheridan if he would like to have a drink of Scotch, and he said sure, so we drank our Scotch and looked at the creek, and it was a beautiful evening, but I'd just left the bottle out, you know, thought nothing of it, and I looked over and sure enough he polished off that pint of Scotch too."

Anderson was forty-two when his book was published in 1978, but his health was already failing. A back injury in 1971 prevented him from further climbing (and likely other forms of adventuring), and in the late 1970s, emphysema drove Anderson into pulmonary exile. He wintered with his grandmother Hazel in Las Vegas and spent summers in the arid clime of Chiloquin, Oregon, at a cabin he christened Visqueen Manor, apparently because it was perpetually in some stage of remodel or disrepair. There he fished the Sprague and Williamson Rivers and even shared his cabin with pioneering fly-tyer and fellow eccentric Polly Rosborough.

Sadly, in 1984, while in Las Vegas, Anderson suffered an attack of emphysema and passed away.

"I just never met anyone else like him," said Amato.

The *Manifesto* was Anderson's only book, but Amato said it has sold approximately three hundred thousand copies, making it Frank Amato Publications' all-time best seller and a contender for the most popular fly-fishing book in modern history. Amato said it remains popular, but I've met many young anglers who have no awareness of it. This doesn't bother me much. I'd classify the *Manifesto* as a must read, but its cult status is a big part of its appeal.

It'd be disingenuous of me to say that I miss Sheridan Anderson. I was just a kid when he died—had never even caught a fish on a fly. But I think Anderson could have filled a role in today's fly-fishing culture, one that's presently vacant—that of the literary catbird, devil's advocate, unflinching reality checker.

"One of the chief chroniclers of the foibles, vanities and pretensions of the period"—that's how climbing author Royal Robbins described Anderson and his coverage of Yosemite's climbing scene. Outdoor photographer Ed Cooper, Anderson's former roomie, said, "I never met anyone who could do what Sheridan could do. He could put a person's personality right into a sketch."

Anderson didn't lampoon the fly-fishing scene the way he poked fun at the Camp 4 climbing scene, though, sure, he drew a goofy likeness of a fly-fishing President Jimmy Carter on page 7 of the *Manifesto*, and there's even one of Frank Amato himself on page 20.

"I'm the Clackamas Cuckoo!" Amato told me, laughing. "I used to smoke a pipe. I guess Sheridan thought I should be in the book."

And unlike much of that period's fly-fishing culture, the *Manifesto*'s aesthetic is distinctly gritty, uncivilized, stripped of affectation. Anderson is the original trout bum. He took the dirtbag lifestyle perfected by the American climbing scene and applied it to fly-fishing.

On page 2 of the *Manifesto*, Anderson renounces the instructional fly-fishing literature of his day as "highly overwritten," claiming "most anglers learn to fish in spite of the textbooks, rather than because of them." That's as close as Anderson gets to hauling anybody to the woodshed, but I'm sure if he had continued to write fly-fishing books, few would have escaped his withering caricaturist's gaze.

"Maybe he'd've done a cartoon about trying to buy waders these days," Amato mused, chuckling. "Some old guy with knobby knees buying a pair of thousand-dollar Patagonia waders."

What would Anderson have said about the sniffy, fedora-wearing patricians of fly-fishing's *A River Runs Through It* period? What would he think of today's brand ambassadors and Instagram bigshots who pick up a flyrod not so much to fish but instead to be photographed and drone-ographed, fishing for likes, shares, and follows?

That is what I miss about Sheridan Anderson—all the cartoons he did not draw, the books he did not write, the pretensions he never skewered.

On the final page of the *Manifesto*, Anderson raises the question his readers likely ask as they close the book: "Is there really a Curtis Creek?"

Anderson replies, "Possibly, my darlings, quite possibly; but I will say no more because that is your final lesson: to go forth and seek your own Curtis Creek—a delightful, unspoiled stretch of water that you will cherish above all others.…There are few Curtis Creeks in this life so when you find it, keep its secret well…"

Had I never stumbled on the real Curtis Creek, I would have found some other Curtis Creek, and the actual Curtis Creek isn't my "own" Curtis Creek, anyway. Paradoxically, another creek holds that distinction. So, I heeded Anderson's final lesson, but I failed the final test—I didn't keep the secret of Curtis Creek, having since fished there with many of my fly-fishing buddies and family members. And now I've even drawn a map to it. So, I apologize to Anderson. Some places are too extraordinary to keep completely secret. (But I think he knew that.)

Nowadays, I search for Anderson's shaggy, hulking ghost on my home water streams—the Blacksmith Fork and the Logan—but most of all Curtis Creek. Despite his generous dimensions, Anderson was apparently quite capable of making himself small when stalking trout. Most of his cartoons depict the main character (a merciless, chubby self-caricature) fly-casting while kneeling, crouching or down on all fours. And now I *am* speaking in a misty, metaphysical way: I have seen Sheridan Anderson many times on Curtis Creek, pirate hat on head and draped in trademark cape, creeping up on the best pools, throwing old-fashioned steeple casts and Curtis Creek sneaks.

14

THE AUDITION

When a newcomer is invited to fish with a group of anglers who've already fished together, it might seem like more than just a fishing trip. To the newcomer, I mean. The performance, evaluation and rendered judgement might make it feel like an audition.

I took a trip like that to Wyoming. There were three of them and one of me.

First, there was Paul, a fish biologist with the Utah Division of Wildlife Resources. Paul was a tall, affable midwesterner. I'd met him a few times but so had every other angler I knew—Paul was known throughout the region for his river and trout conservation work.

Next was Jim, another fish biologist. He worked for Trout Unlimited and had likewise spearheaded many stream conservation projects. With his blocky beard and shock of black hair, Jim bore a slight resemblance to a young Abraham Lincoln. I knew Jim, too, but I never thought I'd ever fish with him—he was as famous if not more so than Paul.

Then came Tyler, who was not a fish biologist at the time but was studying to be one and in the meantime happened to be a fishing guide of some acclaim. Tyler was stocky and talkative, with a face so boyish that I initially underestimated his age by ten years.

Lastly, there was me, newcomer guy. My credentials? Well, I fly-fished—at times. Why had I been invited? I figured some angler of superior caliber had passed away unexpectedly, and the need for a replacement had grown urgent. Jim was kind enough to not specify. I didn't care. This was new, unknown trout water, a tributary of the Bear River.

"This was new, unknown trout water, a tributary of the Bear River."

"It's one of the few places in the watershed where you can catch fluvial Bonneville cutts," said Jim. "Sixteen to twenty inches. Some bigger." That was all I needed to hear.

Fluvial trout are those whose life history involves migration from a large mainstem river up into smaller tributaries for spawning. These far-roving trout grow larger and stronger than trout that remain resident in a single stream. Fluvial Bonnevilles are scarce in the Bear River watershed because human-made obstructions such as dams prevent the fish from moving freely between the mainstem and tributaries. Fluvial trout are found only where a healthy section of the Bear connects to a healthy, high-elevation tributary—and that's where we were going.

I had several concerns. These other three guys had all fished the stream before. Furthermore, Jim said we'd be swinging big, articulated streamers, which wasn't my favorite technique (by which I mean I wasn't very good at it). This is to say nothing of my nasty tailing loop and a track record of getting conspicuously skunked on trips where the fishing was supposed to be superb. I'd even been accused once of being a bad luck charm.

Nevertheless, I made the long drive over obscure state highways and up a twisting, kidney-busting packed-earth road to the stream. It was late June.

We arrived at our campsite just after ten in the morning. As we broke out our waders and flyrods, I heard Tyler talking to Paul about their previous trip to the stream, where they'd landed fish bigger than twenty inches. Soon they were coolly assessing me, asking where I fished, like the small-talk before a job interview. To burnish my credentials, I tried divulging some of the top-secret waters where I fished.

I asked them, "You guys ever go to—" and I named one of my top-secret spots.

Paul nodded impassively. Tyler shrugged and said, "Fish there all the time."

I hastily dropped the names of a couple other places. They remained unmoved, but that was the entirety of the top-secret fishing spots I knew about.

Fortunately, Paul and Tyler soon had their flyrods set up and waders on. Being the first to make ready, Paul got to choose between the upstream and downstream sections. He claimed the downstream section, which could only mean it was the more productive of the two.

Jim attempted to coordinate our itinerary while we were still together. "So, should we meet up back here for dinner?" he asked. "Or for lunch? Do we know where we want to fish tonight?"

But Paul and Tyler were practically fishing already, standing alongside Paul's truck and reaching for the door handles. Paul muttered, "Sure. Yeah." Then they left.

When we'd suited up, Jim and I got into my truck and headed for the upstream section. Jim pointed and said, "Let's start here and leapfrog each other down to where Paul and Tyler are. That should take us most of the day."

"Sounds perfect," I said, not knowing if it really did or not.

There were no trails, so we plunged into the dense brush that flanked the stream. Whippy branches zinged on our waders and slapped our faces. We circled and backtracked through the brush, holding up our rods like radio aerials to keep them from tangling. It took forever to push through, but I feigned nonchalance, as though catching fish was something that interested me only slightly.

It felt like the audition was off to a bad start. Paul and Tyler had a lengthy lead, had fished the stream before and were fishing better water. I hadn't even gotten a good look at the stream.

When at last we reached the water's edge, we found a magnificent trout stream meandering gently through willow brakes and pine thickets. The stream channel was seldom wider than ten yards, but each bend enwrapped a deep, enticing pool. The fast, shallow water was ever-so-slightly milky, while the deeper, slower water was teal and indigo. Undercut banks and overhanging brush brooded above innumerable shady hiding places.

I left Jim and hiked one hundred yards downstream, stationing myself at the upstream end of a bend. Then I cast a tungsten-head streamer across the channel and mended the line furiously. The streamer vanished into the shadowy indigo of the bend. I didn't want to miss the day's first bite to inattention, so as the fly passed through the bottom of the swing, I readied myself for a heavy tug. But the streamer surfaced unmolested at the far end.

I shrugged and repeated the cast, this time mending even more furiously. I was again alert to a strike, but no strike came. It went on like that for a few bends. After about thirty minutes, Jim came up behind me.

"Anything?" he asked. From his dire cheerfulness I inferred he'd already been catching fish.

"Nah," I replied, "not even a bite. Am I doing this right?" I shot a cast across the channel and mended the line. The bend was as blue as the heart of a massive sapphire. The streamer swam into it.

"Yeah," said Jim, "that's the same as I'm doing."

My streamer emerged, again unbothered.

I gestured testily at the bend. "Shouldn't there be a fish in there?"

"Yeah," said Jim with a chuckle, "looks perfect. But like I said, these are fluvial fish. They don't have the density of resident fish. I haven't caught any yet, either. Maybe they're moving back downstream already."

I was relieved to hear this (the part about the density, not that Jim hadn't caught any). It seemed the audition wasn't a complete disaster (yet), so I told Jim I'd skip two big bends downstream to try again.

"Sure," he replied merrily, waving me forward. "Don't worry. We'll start hooking 'em here soon."

I came to a riffle running between overhanging banks and trailed the streamer into the best-looking seams, trying to avoid letting my focus lapse the way it often did on such days of slow fishing. No fish came to the fly, so I crossed the riffle and cast from that side. The fly drifted into a dark lie beneath a hedge of willows with boughs that trailed in the current. No strike. I sighed and let the streamer drift a little farther down so that it wouldn't hook the willows as I retrieved it. And that's when something hit the fly.

The strike had surprised me after all, but the fish came tight anyway and gave me several minutes of panic by running into some heavy current. I stumbled after him, reeling in my slack. Then I ferried him across the channel and banked him on a gravel bar. It was a fluvial Bonneville cutthroat just shy of eighteen inches.

Fluvial Bear River Bonneville cutthroat trout. *Courtesy of Tyler Coleman.*

Fluvial trout are sought after mainly because they grow larger than resident trout; most anglers would rather catch a twenty-inch cutthroat than a ten-inch one. But there is something more beguiling about fluvial Bonnevilles than their size. They are elusive relics, descendants of the indigenous cutthroat population that once superabounded throughout the watershed.

I'd just hooked a second cutthroat when Jim caught up to me again. I reported my catch and showed off the shaky photos I'd shot. Jim still hadn't caught a fish, but he grinned and said, "Guess they're still up here."

I'm not a big fan of scorekeeping while fishing. It feels self-important. Plus, it makes it hard to exaggerate later on. I did feel good to at least be on the scoreboard, but even so, I'd caught fewer than one fish per hour, meaning I could fish until midnight without breaking into double digits. Despite its remoteness and lack of angling pressure, this stream was not easy to fish. Many of the insanely promising pools produced no trout, and I spooked several lunkers from spots where I was sure no sensible fish would hide out.

By the end of the day, I'd managed to catch seven fluvial cutthroats in the upstream section. It wasn't a remarkable number, but I hadn't been skunked, and I hadn't brought bad luck to anyone. Jim caught only two or three, likely because he'd yielded so much good water to me. I think he also spent much of the day inspecting the stream in an official capacity—he'd completed many stream-improvement projects in the vicinity. It was the only way streams like this could remain in existence—constant coordination, negotiation and cooperation between landowners, government agencies and the public.

We returned to our campsite around five o'clock, and I prepared for the tallying of totals and final evaluation that was to come. For reasons that should be obvious, I'd brought enough cold beer and Louisiana hot links for everyone. After distributing these blandishments, I took a seat by the firepit. Paul sat next to me and offered me a cigar. I don't smoke, but I debated whether I should maybe start.

He lit his cigar and champed it contemplatively before asking, "So, how was it?"

"Great," said Jim.

"It was all right," I hedged. "I only caught seven—but they were all phenomenal."

"Well," said Paul, "that's as many as anyone else caught."

I turned to face him. "Seriously?"

Paul nodded. "Yeah, I think I'm at five."

"I got six," said Tyler with a shrug.

For ten fleeting seconds, the scoreboard showed that I had outfished the three of them. I mean there's nothing *intrinsically* wrong with scorekeeping. But then Tyler offhandedly mentioned that they'd caught multiple fish over twenty inches, whereas none of mine exceeded nineteen. I inwardly conceded that even one twenty-inch Bonneville cutthroat trout, wild and native, was enough to offset my narrow numerical lead, and I was mentally recalculating our standings when it dawned on me that all my fussing over catch totals was immaterial and maybe even somewhat gauche to Paul and Jim and Tyler. They didn't care, they didn't regard me as a newcomer and there had been no audition.

Apparently, it was just a fishing trip.

I exhaled and settled into my camp chair. We ate the hot links and drank the beer and made plans to go back and fish until dark.

Jim had, of course, already let me know there was no need for tallies and totals—it was early that afternoon, when he'd caught up to me after I'd hooked my first couple fish. But I hadn't been listening. I'd allowed my focus to lapse.

"Pretty amazing," Jim had said. He looked downstream and trailed one hand in the current. "A stream like this—cold, basically pristine, high-functioning, mainstem-connected, with fluvial cutts."

I could have caught one trout or twenty-one. It didn't matter.

"Not many streams like this," Jim added. "And it just goes on for miles."

15.

TRESPASS FLATS

I've only ever been busted for fishing-related trespass once. It wasn't intentional (well, not *flagrantly*), and I was not arrested or even scolded, really, but it's not something I'm eager to repeat.

Back then, my buddy Jason and I had this big problem: we'd fished all over the Bear River watershed, plumbing the streams we considered most remote and secret—Curtis Creek, Cinnamon Creek and others I don't care to mention. And we were sick of them all.

Every spot was overfished, passé. After a day of poor fishing, instead of blaming ourselves, we'd gripe, "This place is discovered. It's over with."

I'm not saying that was actually true. The Bear River watershed is home to unbeatable trout water. And there were sensational waterways nearby—the Green, the Missouri, the Wind Rivers. But Jason and I had convinced ourselves that we needed a new fix close to home, one which wouldn't require travel days, backpacks or sleeping on the ground. So, when our friend Tim King told us the headwaters section of the Blacksmith Fork not only offered exceptional fishing but was also practically unknown to local anglers, we thought we'd found it.

The Blacksmith Fork is truly a great American trout stream, regionally famous for its designation as a blue-ribbon trout fishery. But that was part of the problem—everyone fished there, and not just locals. Also, despite the blue-ribbon, Blacksmith Fork trout seldom grew very large and most were brown trout rather than locally favored cutthroats.

Tim said the headwaters were different, a Shangri-La of big, wild, native trout, and because it was almost completely surrounded by private property, no one knew about it.

"But ya can't fish there anymore," grumbled Tim with a dismissive wave. "It's all fenced off, posted." He hadn't been there since the 1980s. "Didn't used to be, but it is now."

Jason and I consulted our maps, and, as Tim had lamented, there was no easy way to get there. This is not uncommon in the West. A recent study by the Theodore Roosevelt Conservation Partnership and mapping tech start-up onX revealed that sixteen million acres of public land in the United States are landlocked within private holdings. Laws regarding access to landlocked streams vary by state. In Montana, for example, you can float and wade in streams flowing through private property, provided you enter and exit the water via public land. In Colorado, you can float through private property, but you can't stop or wade.

Utah's stream access laws are currently among the West's most restrictive, but it wasn't always like that. In fact, everything used to be, like, very casual. Landowners did not routinely challenge the public's right to wade or float rivers running through private property until the year 2000.

In June of that year, Kevin and Jodi Conatser were fishing the Weber River. They'd gotten into the river with a rubber raft at a public access point and were floating through private property owned by a family named Johnson. At the time, the right to float through private property was generally acknowledged, arising from the public trust doctrine found in Article 20, Section 1 of the Utah Constitution, which states all lands of Utah "shall be held in trust for the people," and Article 17, Section 1, which states, "All existing rights to the use of any of the waters in this State for any useful or beneficial purpose, are hereby recognized and confirmed."

The act of walking on and touching the streambed was another matter—at best an open question. But that's what the Conatsers were doing—getting out of their raft periodically to fish—against the wishes of the Johnsons.

Court documents describe a "long-running dispute between the Johnsons and the Conatsers." At least twice previously the Johnsons told the Conatsers to get off their property; twice they'd refused. This time, however, the Johnsons had called the law, and a Morgan County sheriff's deputy ticketed the Conatsers for criminal trespass.

The county justice court found the Conatsers guilty, but Utah's Second District Court dismissed the charges on appeal, citing "uncertainty regarding the Conatsers' status as trespassers." Put another way, the court acknowledged the Conatser's right to float through private property but refused to rule regarding the trickier issue of touching the streambed. The Conatsers could have walked away victorious, but instead they filed a civil action requesting partial summary judgment regarding their rights as anglers on the Weber River. The Johnsons filed a cross-motion for essentially the same purpose.

It seems unlikely that either party was aware they were igniting a firestorm that would engulf every fly angler and trout stream in Utah for the next twenty years, but then again, maybe that's exactly what they intended.

In an acrimonious legal slugfest, the Conatsers claimed the right to "recreate in natural public waters," which included floating the Weber through private property and "the right to touch or walk upon the bottoms of said waters in non-obtrusive ways."

The court ruled that the Conatsers were indeed entitled to float the Weber through private property, but they could not touch the streambed unless it was incidental to their right of floatation—they could touch bottom to navigate and avoid hazards, but they couldn't anchor or disembark to fish.

One can only presume here that the trout in the contested stretch of the Weber grew to obscene proportions, because the Conatsers immediately appealed to the Utah Supreme Court.

And they won.

In 2008, in *Conatser v. Johnson*, the Utah Supreme Court unanimously upheld a broad public easement on Utah streams, which allowed the public "to (1) engage in all recreational activities that utilize the water and (2) touch privately owned beds of state waters in ways incidental to all recreational rights provided for in the easement." The Conatsers weren't just victorious, but they'd also won big for all Utah anglers.

This was important to Jason and me because routes to access Tim's Shangri-La were few. The first and worst came in from the east on cryptic Forest Service trails at a distance of ten miles—way too far to hike for an afternoon of fishing. The second route was from the west, a hike of just two miles up a dirt road that penetrated the private property, but we didn't know whether that was a Forest Service road (and therefore a public right-of-way) or a *decommissioned* Forest Service road (and therefore private property).

The last and best way to the landlocked headwaters was the simplest: step into the upper Blacksmith Fork from public land, wade upstream through the private property, emerge onto the public land of the headwaters and then fish our asses off. And the *Conatser* decision had granted us the easement we needed to do it that way.

But we were too late.

The *Conatser* easement survived for only two years. The victory was a pyrrhic one. Because, far from settling the matter, the Utah Supreme Court's decision opened numerous new disputes about boundary fencing, navigability, high-water marks and the main question: Who holds title to a streambed?

So, while Jason and I were obtusely consulting outdated USGS topos, Utah's legislature—a parliament of real estate developers—quietly passed a bill that not only gutted *Conatser* by limiting streambed contact to incidental touching, but it also restricted public access to *navigable waters only*, thereby extinguishing access rights tacitly acknowledged by landowners before 2000.

Signed into law in spring 2010, the hilariously titled Public Waters Access Act forbade Jason and me from wading upstream through the Blacksmith Fork to reach Shangri-La. Instead, we'd have to rely on one of the remaining ground routes, both of which were problematic—one legally sketchy and the other necessitating backpacks and sleeping on the ground. The Blacksmith Fork headwaters were practically in our backyard, but the Public Waters Access Act made it as distant as a stream in Montana.

So, early that summer we decided to use the two-mile dirt road. We called this the Forest Service road because we hoped that's what it was. We weren't sure. One map showed it was publicly accessible; another didn't show it at all. We asked around, but half-heartedly, because we didn't really want to know for sure. We just wanted a way in, if for only a day, to see if it was still how Tim had described it.

The Forest Service road was gated, but there were no no-trespassing signs. And the gate was locked, but it was equipped with climb-over steps, and the lock was of handsome brushed brass with "U.S." stamped on it.

"This has got to be Forest Service," declared Jason.

We clambered diffidently over the gate and skulked down the road. We saw lots of cattle but no ranchers or deputy sheriffs. After hiking for a mile, it felt like maybe we were safe.

Then an old farm truck came into view.

It was clattering down another dirt road an eighth of a mile away, but even at that distance, we knew the driver had seen us. His window was down, and he turned his face to us, then to the road, then us.

"Welp, that's it," I muttered.

"Chill, dude," said Jason. "We're just here to fish. We thought it was a Forest Service road."

The truck came closer. We kept walking. The driver looked again from the road to us, but then he raised his hand into the air and waved. We grinned and waved back, and the truck rattled on out of sight.

Then we exhaled and entered Shangri-La.

But it wasn't like Tim had said. It was a lot better.

The stream descended through hilly sylvan groves like a myth and then meandered augustly across grassy parklands. There were corrals and fences, but we saw not a single other person. As foretold, the fish were big and easy to catch, and they were cutthroats with rich backcountry coloration—fluorescent blush on bronze flanks and electric-white throats inlaid with fuchsia slashes.

Every good bend and riffle produced a couple of fish; many pools held five or six, and the best water might harbor a lurking pool captain, a big heavy cutt with a prerogative to rise before his nearby subordinates.

Tim said the place was named Mullein Hollow for its population of European mullein, a nonnative medicinal plant that produces flowering stalks up to six feet tall. Certain maps confirmed this. However, that's not what Jason and I called it. Neither did we call it the Shangri-La of Trout.

We called it Trespass Flats—not because we suspected ourselves of trespassing; we knew we weren't. After that first furtive trip, we returned every few days, boldly vaulting the gate, strutting down the Forest Service road and generally making ourselves to home. When ranchers appeared, we waved at them, and they waved back.

I was only dimly aware of Utah's stream-access laws before the legislative skullduggery of 2010 and seldom concerned myself with private property. But after the passage of the Public Waters Access Act and our discovery of Trespass Flats, I formed the retroactive indignation of the little kid who wants to play with a toy only because some other kid is playing with it.

The Utah Stream Access Coalition, a nonprofit legal group, had also formed in response to the Public Waters Access Act, but unlike me, it had been monitoring threats to the Public Trust since *Conatser*. I've heard the group called "fly-fishing hippie lawyers," and there is utility in that description—its objective is to undo the disaster of the Public Waters Access Act and restore Utah streams to the Public Trust.

It hasn't been easy. In 2010, it challenged the constitutionality of the Public Waters Access Act in Utah's Fourth District Court, asserting that the public's right to fish a four-mile stretch of the Provo River had been curtailed by private property owners. Chris Barkey, one of the coalition's original board members, told me the war began on the Provo because "people had a sense that they lost something there, something they wanted back."

In 2012, the court ruled that the Public Waters Access Act was in fact unconstitutional. Some public access was restored, but the property owners,

Victory Ranch Acquisitions, appealed the case to the Utah Supreme Court, where it languished until 2019, only to be remanded to the lower court on a technicality, where it remains lodged today.

"That's ten years of my life I'm never getting back," Barkey remarked.

But the hippie lawyers have won battles too. In May 2011, they set their sights on a one-mile stretch of the Weber River flowing through private property, again claiming that a property owner, Orange Street Development, divested the public of their right to access the stream. This time the coalition stayed within the framework of the Public Waters Access Act, arguing in Utah's Third District Court that because the Weber was a navigable waterway at the time of Utah statehood, the public held title to its streambed, according to the law itself.

In 2015, the court again ruled in the coalition's favor, and Orange Street appealed. The coalition dropped the claim to streambed title, but in November 2017, the Utah Supreme Court issued a decision upholding most of the Third District's ruling: the public had unlimited access to the streambed—in that one-mile stretch. The same became true by extension for another thirty-nine miles of the river, and suddenly, the full *Conatser* easement was restored—but only to that forty miles of the Weber River.

Barkey acknowledged the win but again expressed a latent dissatisfaction.

"We messed up the Weber case," he confessed. "We should have gone for title. We were trying to play nice, play fair. We messed up."

When I asked him about the future of Utah stream access, Barkey replied with choleric equanimity.

"All these bigger rivers are going to be found to be navigable," he insisted. "The Logan, the Blacksmith, the Ogden—they'll all be ruled navigable, and property owners are going to lose rights, but people [the public] just aren't okay with violating the Public Trust."

At Trespass Flats, the fishing just got better as we headed into late July. Jason and I achieved our initial success with nothing but our own small-stream aptitude, which was merely adequate. The trout deserved most of the credit. But as we figured out the best flies, approach angles and big-fish hideouts, we had our best-ever days on the Blacksmith Fork, a distinction that stands to this day.

Then, one evening after catching an appalling abundance of Trespass cutthroats on tan-and-fudge foam hoppers, we were walking back down the Forest Service road when a lady on a four-wheeler intercepted us. She wore battered coveralls and regarded us with a hard, weathered face.

She fixed us with a flinty glare and said, "What're you doing here?"

"Just fishing on the Forest land," I drawled, jabbing a thumb over my shoulder.

"No," she snapped. "I mean what're you doing *here*. On this *road*."

I intended to reply, "This is a Forest Service right-of-way." But I only made it to the *f* sound.

"No, it *isn't*," she interrupted. "It is *not*."

To this I meant to reply, "Well, look, it's not posted, and there's a Forest Service lock on the gate, and at least one Forest Service map says it's public, and a guy in the Fish and Wildlife told us he thought it might be, too, so, you can see what we were thinking."

But instead Jason jumped in and answered, "Okay, we'll go ahead and leave and we won't come back. Sorry to bother you." The lady watched without another word as we departed.

Later that summer, Jason and I used GIS map layers (new technology then) to decipher the checkerboard of public and private land and find a legal route to Trespass Flats. This one was only six miles long but without a trail. So, in the end, we had to backpack in after all—six miles overland—to fish a public stretch of our own homewaters. The ideal route to Trespass Flats was and still is wading upstream through the private property, but the courts have yet to rule if that's permissible.

"It'll be two years before we hear anything on the Provo case," Barkey told me. "But keep in mind the Provo case isn't about the Provo; it's about every stream in the state. The evidence for navigability is there. So, whether we win or lose every lawsuit, the access will be restored, and then it'll come down to legislation both sides can live with. Or we all just go back into court. The mentality has to change. We need understanding and respect from all sides."

16

BLOOMINGTON

L et me say up front that it wasn't much to look at. Bloomington Creek crept down off the mountain like a spooky, mistreated kid. It skulked along its eroded channel, running quietly beneath deadfall and around the thick trunks of haunted junipers.

You could tell Bloomington had once been a proud little trout stream. You could squint your eyes and picture it coursing cold and clear through dark primeval timber stands and out into the endless fecund marshland of the sprawling Bear Lake ecosystem.

That was, of course, before the clear-cutting and irrigation, before the sheep and sugar beets. And it was before the Bear River was sliced open by water developers in the early twentieth century and bled into Bear Lake.

Like the Bear River itself, Bloomington Creek is now a working waterway, little more than a muddy ditch, trampled and neglected, notable mostly for the acre-feet it contributes to the surrounding agrarian economy.

To get to Bloomington Creek, Tim Keller and I drove up Center Street in Bloomington, Idaho, which consisted of a one-room U.S. Post Office, twenty or so houses squatting along a dozen tiny intersecting streets without curb or gutter, and in the middle of it a sheriff's deputy who sat in his prowler making sure nobody exceeded the speed limit. It was a post–Labor Day Sunday afternoon, and from what I could tell, Keller's big GMC truck constituted the sole automobile traffic for twenty miles in every direction. But the deputy was on the case anyhow. He watched us but let us pass, so we continued onto a jeep road that climbed out the back of the town and up into the mountains right behind the houses. The jeep road followed the creek. We were heading up to Bloomington Lake.

On account of heavy livestock grazing, the whole mountainside had a weird, manicured look. The vegetation was nibbled down to the dirt. The grass looked like plastic miniature golf turf, the kind my grandma pasted onto the steps of her porch for traction. There were cows in every direction. I saw eroded canals and silted-in irrigation diversions.

"So, clearly not managed for recreation," I said to Keller as I craned my neck to see the creek from the passenger seat.

"Not really managed at all," answered Keller.

We stopped to check out the creek.

"I can't fish this," I said, approaching the thin trickle. "There's no fish in this water. There's no water in this stream. And there's cow shit everywhere."

But Keller had already wandered off, probably looking for deer. I stood there talking to myself. Cowpies as big as manhole covers lay on the road, along the creek, in the creek, washing down the creek.

"I can't fish this," I repeated.

Then I noticed a handful of fish holding in the slow outflow of a blasted-out old beaver pond. I thought they were probably cutthroats, but at that distance, it was hard to say. They were just dark elongated ovals holding steady in the laminar outflow. The only reason I even spotted them was that one broke ranks, plucked a morsel of forage from the flow and waggled back into formation. The movement had caught my eye. If I could get a fly on that moving water, I'd hook one. I tried getting closer but was barred by a thicket of whited willow bones. There was no way to cover the fish from my side of the pond, not even with my tenkara rod. I might be able to hike around and cast across to them from the far side, but then it'd be a long, long shot with no backcast. I could come at them from upstream if I wanted to crawl on my belly through ten yards of cow shit and probably spook them anyway.

"Screw this," I said, and I plowed like a hippo into the dead willow thicket. If I couldn't catch the fish, I'd at least find out what kind they were. The dead branches clattered dryly, slapping my waders as I crashed through to the margins of the pond.

To my great surprise, they were cutthroats. They scattered as soon as I got close, but I saw them—cutthroats.

We drove to another spot. Here the creek ran down a steep grade through gnarly timber and out onto a wide flat swale where it split into channels. But there were no reeds or rushes along the banks. It was just yards and yards of the same clipped-down vegetation, a miniature golf course in the middle of the woods. The cows had eaten everything and left their shit behind like gigantic quiche Lorraines baked rancid in the sun.

A few of the channels looked almost deep enough to hold a fish, but I didn't catch any. Some of the channels held just a film of water clinging to the bed so shallow that the hook of my dry fly snagged the bottom while still floating on the water.

I crossed the swale and moved up into the timber. Keller was off somewhere looking for the deer. Among the trees it felt a little wilder. Birds quarreled in the canopy. I saw a muskrat and what might have been fox scat. A faint footpath wound through grass that had managed to establish itself sparsely among the deadfall where the cows couldn't graze. Here the whole creek ran in one main channel again.

Casting was difficult, the lanes full of juniper boughs and dead leaning trees. It was like casting in the showroom of a ladder factory. I made slingshot casts and little half-roll casts and dapped the fly onto the water. I didn't catch anything. Farther upstream, the creek became narrow and incised, three feet deep and not even that wide, so channelized that it made the echoey gurgle of a flowing sewer.

I came to a log footbridge about as big around as a man's leg. The log had lain there for so long the ground had absorbed it. The creek narrowed there. The water backed up as it approached the log and then shot out noisily downstream. Figuring the spot should provide physical and hydraulic cover for at least one good fish, I cast a blond Elk Hair Caddis to the bridge. First, I cast from the downstream side, trying to sail the fly between the log and the water. No fish. I crossed over the stream and crept upstream past the bridge and cast downstream to the narrow place. No fish. I even let the fly float under the bridge and on down a few feet. I continued up the drainage.

If you want to get technical about it, it's the South Fork of Bloomington Creek I'm talking about. It drains out of Bloomington Lake at an elevation of nearly six thousand feet on the eastern side of the Bear River Mountains, maybe a mile from the east-west divide of the range. The jeep road continues almost all the way up to the lake. You just have to park and walk the final half-mile or so. The South Fork of Bloomington Creek meets up with the Middle Fork and North Fork a couple miles downstream to form Bloomington Creek proper and then runs down the mountain, over the irrigation structures, past the sheriff's deputy's prowler, under U.S. Highway 89 and out into the vast marshy expanse of what is now the Bear Lake National Wildlife Refuge, where it empties cryptically and

Bloomington Creek.

diffusely into Mud Lake, the appendix to Bear Lake, which attaches to the Bear River via Stewart Dam and the input and output canals.

Thus Bloomington Creek connects anthropogenically to the greater Bear River watershed, indirectly contributing its nonpoint fecal coliforms and fertilizer pollutants to the entire system. Bloomington Creek, like scores of other tributary streams, falls under the provisions of the Bear River Compact, that antiquated and byzantine interstate commerce agreement between Utah, Idaho and Wyoming, which not only boldly epitomizes the sanctimonious despotism for which western water law is widely known but is also so tedious and impenetrable that it makes the management of certain synthetically derived financial instruments like mortgage-backed securities seem positively elementary by comparison.

And the compact upholds and maintains this Faustian arrangement in perpetuity, renewing itself every twenty years and entitling a select few commercial entities to control decadent amounts of Bear River water. The compact in particular and western water law in general do not consider Bloomington Creek as a trout stream so much as a revenue stream. Even if someone had the wherewithal to remove the cattle and close the irrigation diversions, western water law makes it illegal to allow all of the stream's water to flow to its terminus.

Upstream from the footbridge, I finally caught a few cutthroats, none longer than my hand and all still sporting par marks. Sunlight filtered down through the trees, and the fish lying in my palm shone like a cloisonné brooch, finely wrought jewelry in a boutique strewn with cowpies.

Upstream from there, it was too brushy and timber-fallen to cast, so I turned and walked downstream to find the road. Keller had probably finished cataloguing the deer in the vicinity and would be ready to continue up the jeep road to the lake.

Bloomington wasn't much to look at, but it was something to think about. It was strangled by irrigation, trampled by agriculture, disregarded by water law. Like so many other waterways in the West, it was perhaps too small and too far gone to consider with any real conservational urgency.

And yet it supported trout. What would it look like if this stream were restored, taken care of, cared for?

As I approached the footbridge again, I took a hard look at it from a distance of one hundred feet. The blond Elk Hair Caddis was waterlogged and fish-slimed by this time. It wouldn't float even if I'd wanted it to, so I put it on the water and it sank as it drifted down. When the fly got under the bridge, I lifted my rod tip and held the fly in place. It tumbled and dragged in the turbulence of the narrowed channel just a couple inches below the surface. There came a metallic flash, and I set the hook on a fine cutthroat of a pound or so.

17.

SUMMER OF BILL

One morning in early July, I got a text from Bill. He told me he wanted to take his boat out on Daniels Reservoir to fish for the big rainbow trout.

"My wife says I'm too old to take the boat out by myself," Bill texted. "Are you interested? I prefer to go during the week but can be flexible on that. Is there a day that works for you?"

Daniels is a reservoir of about one square mile on the Little Malad River in Idaho. It has a long-standing artificials-only regulation, barbless-hook rule and slot limit. I'd heard it was squirming with trophy rainbows. I'd never fished there before, but I sure as hell wanted to.

I tried not to sound too eager. "Yeah, Bill, I could probably take a day off and maybe head out with you."

A few more texts, and we'd agreed on a Tuesday one week hence.

Bill texted, "Can you be here at 5:30 sharp?"

"In the morning??" I joked.

"Yes," he replied, "I'd like to get there at 7:00."

Now, if you're going to spend a long day in a small boat with someone, it's important that you both know about sarcasm. It comes in handy if you want to say, "Great cast!" or "Nice fish!" without really meaning it. I was ready to overlook the possibility that Bill was impervious to irony, but there was another, more peculiar problem.

I didn't know Bill. I had no idea who this guy was.

"Sure," I texted back, "5:30 it is."

Daniels Reservoir.

I looked up Bill on social media and was surprised to discover he and I were already friends. However, scrolling through his content only deepened the enigma. There were photos of Wyoming and Arizona and even the Galapagos Islands, but all the fishing photos involved spinning rods and grandkids, and the one close-up photo of Bill himself didn't ring a single bell. Bill and I had no online friends in common, and my real-life friends had never heard of him.

On Monday, Bill texted, "We still on for tomorrow morning at 5:30?"

"Sure, Bill, but let me ask you a question. Who the hell are you?"

That's not what I texted. It was way too late for that.

Instead, I texted, "Yes sir! See you then! Looking forward to it!"

The way that Bill kept dropping our precise start time into his texts suggested I'd better be on time, so I got to his house at 5:25 a.m. It was still dark. Who was this guy? I had to assume Bill's online photo was simply too outdated for me to recognize. Or maybe it was too recent. Or maybe there was something essential but unphotographable about Bill that I'd instantly recall on meeting him face to face.

But it wasn't any of that. I really just didn't know him.

Bill met me out on his driveway. Clean-shaven, dungarees, silver hair, perhaps twenty years my senior. He was friendly. In the glow of a porchlight we shook hands.

"Nice to see you again," said Bill. "It's been a while."

"Yes," I said. "Too long."

I stole glances at Bill as I loaded my gear into his vehicle, worried I'd blow my cover. He fiddled with the tie-down straps on his boat trailer, but everything was already ready and obviously had been since the day before. Then he offered me a cup of coffee, and as soon as we set out on State Highway 30 for Idaho, it was official: I was on an all-day fishing trip with a total stranger.

But the mystery didn't last. I finally confessed. "Bill, I feel embarrassed, but I can't remember how we first met."

He knew he'd had me at a disadvantage from the start, so he chuckled kindly and unriddled the matter. He was a retiree from Arizona who summered in northern Utah—a summer citizen, we called them. Many years earlier, he explained, he'd attended a single Trout Unlimited meeting where I'd made a presentation about fishing on the Blacksmith Fork. After the meeting, Bill had introduced himself and asked me if I wanted to go fishing some time. Then he'd waited something like a decade to follow up.

"I feel bad it's taken this long," said Bill, "but I appreciate you being available."

So began the Summer of Bill. I still didn't really know him, but there was time for that. Once I volunteered to wade in the lake to help untrailer his boat, and after I'd established myself as a capable and *punctual* first mate, Bill would put me on speed dial and we'd be on Daniels hauling in trophy rainbows every few days all summer long. I rested easy in the passenger seat as we crossed into Idaho.

The final leg of the drive zig-zagged over two-lane farm roads and up a canyon almost thirty minutes northwest of the tiny village of Malad, which itself was an hour's drive from its largest neighbor, Pocatello, population of only sixty thousand. So, although the reservoir was surrounded by rolling, dry-farm fields, it felt quite remote.

Bill pointed out the original site of the reservoir, a few miles south of where it is now. The old dam is a hulking ruin of concrete and blackened iron spanning a narrow place in the valley. The faint remnants of the historic shoreline inscribed the hillsides around what is now many acres of cow pasture. I pictured boats gliding across the missing water and soaring over the backs of the grazing cattle.

We reached the boat ramp at 7:00 a.m.

"Hey, we made great time!" beamed Bill.

He backed his boat into the lake. It was a fourteen-foot, riveted aluminum outfit with plastic swiveling seats and an eight-horsepower outboard motor. I waded down the ramp into the water and braced the boat so that Bill could board without getting wet. Then I shoved off and vaulted with a splash into the bow.

The Bear River watershed is home to nearly one hundred reservoirs, most of them on tributaries and most covering a square mile or less. Almost all were constructed for irrigation or hydroelectric power for the sugar beet industry, the economic heart of the region in the late 1800s and early 1900s. Today, these reservoirs are more notable for their nonnative sport-fish species. Porcupine Reservoir in the south of the watershed holds kokanee salmon. Oneida in the north has walleye. Newton has tiger muskie. Cutler holds bass, bullhead, perch and other offspring of illicit "bucket stockings" that go back a century.

As I smelled the outboard motor exhaust and watched the keel parting the glassy water, I recalled a summer camping trip many years before with my sons, Klaus and Shreve, at Newton Reservoir, a lake of just 350 acres on Clarkston Creek. It's one of only two dams in the watershed that is still managed directly by the Bureau of Reclamation. (The other is Hyrum Reservoir.) Our little boat, which we christened the *Aquabat*, drew a shallower draft, but it was functionally identical to Bill's.

Shreve and Klaus were probably eight and ten years old at the time. We'd launched the *Aquabat* at daybreak and caught perch and bass and even a few small tiger muskies. Later in the day, the fishing slowed, but we kept at it, sunburnt and languishing in the broiling aluminum shell. That evening, after Dutch oven chicken for dinner, we took the boat out again with a small electric camping lantern. It wasn't as bright as a real crappie light, but we anchored up in a cove, set one of the oars athwart in the oarlocks and hung the light out over the water from the oar handle.

"Little minnows and baby fish are attracted to bright lights at night," I told the boys. "So, they'll swim up to our light, and hopefully some bigger fish will follow."

The boys cast their jigs, peering over the side with an anticipation indistinguishable from actual fear, unsure of what might emerge from the eerily green glowing water. They didn't have to wait long to find out. Small perch hit the lures right away. Bigger fish followed. I tied on a Woolly Bugger and hooked a sixteen-inch smallmouth. We hooked up doubles and at least one triple. For an hour, scarcely a minute passed when one of us wasn't reeling in a fish. It was the kind of truly abundant fishing that permanently binds young anglers to the sport.

In *The Habit of Rivers*, Ted Leeson asserts, "With a few firm exceptions, fishing from boats holds little appeal. It has a certain industrial quality about it, a no-nonsense fixation on the business of catching fish."

I understand what he means, especially with regard to drift boats. There might never be a more absurdly elaborate and extravagant human contrivance than the drift boat. It is exhaustively engineered and exquisitely manufactured, as expensive as certain factory-new automobiles and built for the exclusive purpose of capturing trout and then immediately letting them go again.

But fishing from an old tin boat like Bill's is something totally unlike other kinds of fishing, something that might feel nostalgic even if you've never done it before. A summer day in such a boat sears itself into memory.

Bill sat in the aft seat wearing a hopeful expression as he steered us to Daniels's northeastern shore. The sun stood a few degrees above the horizon. Bill cut the motor and we glided to a stop. The bank was lined with reeds. Bleached branches of inundated trees rose from the water like skeletal fingers.

Bill pointed at a reef of submerged aquatic vegetation. "Last year about this time, we were catching 'em like crazy on damselfly nymphs all along this line of weeds here."

I didn't see any adult damselflies, but I tied on a damselfly nymph and cast to the weeds. No takers. We tried other flies and nymphs without success. Between guesses about why the fish weren't biting, we spoke of our families and jobs. Like many retired guys, Bill had lots to say about things like the high cost of prescription medications, gasoline and recreational fees. He wasn't nearly old enough to be my grandpa—he was probably younger than my dad—but he was a classic American grandfather: affable (from a polite distance), more avuncular than fatherly and grimly devoted to punctuality despite having no place to be and all day to arrive.

I thought of my grandpa Oscar, who reportedly began teaching me to fish when I was three. His boat was an eighteen-foot fiberglass Hydrodyne with a canvas bimini top, wraparound windshield and teal and white hull trimmed in chrome. It looked more like an amphibious '57 Chevy Bel Air than a fishing outfit, but in that boat among the coves of Arizona's Lake Havasu, Grandpa Oscar taught me to bait a hook, jig for bluegill, troll for stripers and toss top-water poppers to weed beds for smallmouth.

My grandpa's tug of choice was big fat catfish, which he tempted with homemade stinkbait, the recipe for which he evidently guarded so jealously that he took it to his grave rather than passing it on to me, his own protégé. I know, at least, it contained Velveeta, puréed chicken giblets and Jim Beam. Ingredients guessed at based on the stultifying aroma include buttermilk and chewing tobacco. It was mixed in a steel Folger's coffee can and left in the garage to ripen in the Arizona heat, which in summertime started at "pizza oven" and often rose to "equator of planet Mercury." When the bait was sufficiently gangrenous, it took on the purplish black iridescence of congealed motor oil, a noxious biscuit dough with the reek of Limburger cheese.

Bill allowed the boat to drift unanchored to cover more water. When we floated over weeds or shallows, Bill started the motor and backed into open water. Between casts, he furrowed his brow and scanned the water, as though suspecting we were on the wrong lake.

"Not sure why we're not catching 'em," Bill apologized. "Last time, we were hooking nice fish, oh, about every five minutes."

We navigated to a new expanse of water. "Eighteen, nineteen feet deep here," Bill announced, peering at the tiny monochrome monitor of his fish-finder. "Weedy bottom. I'm marking fish down there."

Contrary to my typical attitude, the shortage of fish had yet to occur to me as a crisis. I worked my half of the water in a hot, sleepy daze, casting a wet fly, letting it descend and then lazily retrieving before the fly contacted the weeds—meditating, really. We hooked a few small rainbows. I set down my flyrod and opened a beer. The bottle sweated in the heat. The heat settled into the boat. The boat rocked on the water. The water *glunk*ed against the hull.

Time passed imperceptibly. The sun hung in the heat just beneath its zenith for what seemed like hours. Summertime seeped into my bones. There came to mind a Polaroid I once saw in a photo album belonging to Oscar's sister. This was years ago, but even then the photo was so faded it was mostly pale hues of red and green. I was a toddler in the photo, standing on the prow of Oscar's Hydrodyne, which was nosed up onto a gravelly beach. My grandma, probably in her fifties, stood next to the boat holding up a massive bass she'd caught. She was lipping the fish like a pro, remarkable not because she'd landed it—she was as competent an angler as Oscar—but because although the fish must have weighed ten pounds, she was effortlessly hoisting it high enough to compare its length to my height. The bass was only slightly shorter than I was.

My earliest memory of fishing is a trip with Grandpa Oscar to Kaibab Lake in northern Arizona. I couldn't have been older than six. Like Daniels Reservoir, Kaibab Lake is small and sits high in the mountains. And it holds trout, but at first, nobody caught any. While my grandpa presumably worked methodically through his warmwater arsenal of Rapalas, Rooster Tails and rubber worms, I sat in the back of the boat, occupying myself with a coffee can full of pinyon seeds.

Big red coffee cans figure significantly in my fishing memories—they held not only stinkbait but also nightcrawlers, live baitfish, busted lures Oscar planned to salvage and (in this case) pinyon seeds I'd gathered that morning from around our campsite. I don't recall why I collected them, and I can say even less about why I brought them fishing, but I spent much of that day dropping the seeds one by one over the stern. The water was clear enough to see almost to the bottom. I hunched over the gunwale, my face only a foot above the water, watching each seed spiral down until it didn't so much recede from view as slowly fade away. This was evidently enough to keep me content.

Later on, Grandpa caught a big fish. This is my first recollection of trout. I'd surely seen paintings and photos of trout in outdoor magazines, but there in the boat I could only stare at the sleek, gleaming fish. It lacked the spiny fins, heavy scales and toadish grimace of bass and the other warmwater species I was better acquainted with. Hammocked heavily in the net, the trout flashed prismatically, like a torpedo fashioned from diamonds and chrome.

"That's a rainbow trout," said my grandpa. He didn't have to explain why it was called that.

Bill had planned to fish until two o'clock, but we stayed on the water until four o'clock, waiting for the fish to start biting. They finally did. As the sun declined, the damselflies emerged en force, and the rainbows leaped clear of the water for them. I tied on an adult pattern and hooked a sixteen-inch rainbow. Bill caught several good fish.

But the Summer of Bill ended up being mostly that one trip. I got busy with yardwork. Bill had medical appointments and grandkids. We went back to Daniels that September but then Bill returned to Arizona. This is not to say I was disappointed. Just before we turned for shore, I set my hook on what I knew was a fine rainbow. I locked the flyline under my index finger and hastily reeled in my slack.

"Think this might be a bigger one," I said over my shoulder.

Daniels Reservoir rainbow trout. *Courtesy of Bill Kramer.*

Bill reached for the net. The trout was at first only a silvery blur in the murk two fathoms down. He refused to come up even to leap. I eventually played him to the boat, but he bolted at the sight of the net. I carefully raised him back up, but he went on the drag again when the net reappeared. At last, he jumped, shimmied stiffly in the air for an instant and landed on the water with a clap. Bill got the net under him.

The trout measured half an inch shy of twenty inches, the reservoir's slot-limit. To all appearances, he was the same trout I'd seen on my grandpa's boat that day on Kaibab. The trout glittered blindingly in the sun, and the Summer of Bill seared itself into my memory.

I lifted the rainbow from the net and lowered him into the water. With a lash of his tail, the big trout raised a splash and vanished into the deep.

18

GHOSTS OF MINK CREEK

Tim Keller and I tried for so long to fish together on Mink Creek that we quit believing that it would ever happen. When we finally settled on a Sunday in September, I nearly forgot about it because I figured one of us would bail out.

(Presumably me.)

Keller's a native of tiny Preston, Idaho, but his pioneer ancestors were the original settlers of the even smaller farming village of Mink Creek, which nestles along its watery namesake about fifteen miles north of Preston. The Kellers came west in the 1860s under orders from Mormon prophet Brigham Young, some of the first to settle the region. That was one reason I wanted to fish Mink Creek with Keller. He knew the area as well as or better than anyone living—not only where to catch fish, but (as importantly) how to get at them.

Mink Creek is a modestly sized, spring-fed tributary of the Bear River and is named (as Keller put it) "for the small, fur-bearing animal that prowls its banks." Some of its flow is diverted for irrigation, and it powers a small hydroelectric plant. However, although Mink Creek drains less than thirty square miles and is only twelve miles long, it's unlike many streams in the Bear River watershed—not bogged down in endless ag fields and is for the most part fast and cold and wild. Maybe that's why it's so jealously guarded and haunted by controversy—it's beautiful and largely unspoiled.

Keller and I had fished Mink Creek years earlier, but we'd settled for a lower stretch on private property belonging to one of his relations or neighbors. Keller insisted it was OK to fish there based on some ancient blood oath or gentlemen's agreement, but it felt like a better-to-ask-forgiveness situation to me. I caught some really nice cutthroats, but I kept looking over my shoulder for the sheriff coming to chase us off the water.

Ever since then, I'd been hoping to go back and fish the upper Mink, but even as I loaded my gear into my Tacoma to head for Keller's house, I was skeptical. The headwater spring and first three miles of the stream are on Forest Service land, but that's at the top of Mink Creek Canyon, which is hemmed around by private property. Keller's tales of angry landowners and constabulary entanglements made it sound like the public water was trickier to fish than the private.

Keller's place was a ruthlessly manicured green and white farmhouse. I grabbed my waders to throw into Keller's big GMC pickup, but he checked me at the curb.

"We're gonna need your truck for this trip," he said. "Mine's too big for where we're going. Good thing you've got new tires."

Keller's a big fellow. I felt self-conscious as he crammed himself into the small cab. His knees pressed against the glove box, and his head brushed the roof. It looked like Bruce Banner had climbed in and then transformed into the Incredible Hulk.

He shrugged. "Kind of all right once you get settled," he said as we headed north from Preston.

It bears mentioning that this story ends with a day of superb trout fishing on Mink Creek. It ends with a clear September sky and a series of runs and pools teeming with gullible brook trout ranging in length from ten to thirteen inches. The story ends quite satisfactorily.

But it begins with a padlock.

In the spring of 2006, more than ten years earlier, an out-of-towner named Allen Barber, who'd recently purchased a Mink Creek land parcel known as the Benson Ranch, decided that a decrepit logging road running through the property was nothing but a nuisance. He claimed that scofflaws used the road to trespass, and aside from that, it served no purpose. So, he gated it, clapped a padlock on it, and posted a no trespassing sign.

But this so-called Benson Road was actually owned by Franklin County, Idaho, and was a public right-of-way used to pass through Benson Ranch to access the Forest Service land at the top of the canyon. Residents had been hunting that area, known as the Steeps, for generations, and the only way to drive there was over the Benson Road.

Barber knew he'd ruffle feathers by padlocking that gate. However, he asserted, the Benson Road dead-ended before reaching the Forest Service boundary and, therefore, could not be a public right-of-way. Moreover, Barber reasoned, he had the right to protect his property from the public's impudent trespasses.

He wasn't the only one who felt that way. Mink Creek landowner Lenna Samuel summed it up in her 2006 letter to the editor of the *Preston Citizen*: "Hunters cut your fences if they want to go somewhere else. Gates are always left open. Four wheelers dig gullies in your fields. Lovers leave their undies scattered around our yards....No one asks for permission."

The strain between private property rights and public access seethes continuously just behind the neighborly facade of the West. Only the issue of water rights is more fraught, more incendiary.

In the summer of 2006, Barber took a step further by petitioning Franklin County to vacate the Benson Road, which would permanently cut off the public's vehicle access to the Forest Service land and the upper Mink. It wasn't the first time this had happened—the previous landowner tried the same move two years before. Barber wasn't just ruffling feathers; he was also reigniting a feud that flared up every few years, one in which Tim Keller's father, Leness, fought at the front lines on the side of keeping the road open. Leness had testified before the Franklin County Commission that the Benson Road had been in use by the public for 125 years, and he'd collected signatures from seventy-five locals who wanted to keep using it.

I'd met Leness just once and then only in passing. He was tall and broad, with a lantern jaw and flinty gaze—an imposing figure despite his eighty-three years. I had no trouble imagining him rallying his neighbors against Allen Barber. My impression was that if Leness did something, it stayed done.

As Keller and I approached Mink Creek Canyon that September Sunday, Keller announced that we were going to drive straight up that same contentious right-of-way to access the Mink's public waters.

"Is that the only way to get there?" I asked.

"No," said Keller with a mordant chuckle, "you can come down on foot from the cliffs on the far side—if you've got a goddam parachute."

We turned off the highway onto Mink Creek Road and then onto smaller roads until the way was barred by the very same steel gate Barber had padlocked twelve years before. The occasion felt positively historical. The gate wasn't locked, but it was chained shut. Keller hopped out of the passenger seat to open it, and with a baleful grin, he said, "I have a picture of me standing on the supposedly private property side of this gate, back when it was still locked."

Tim Keller. *Courtesy of Tim Keller.*

It seemed that our trip to Mink Creek was for Keller as much about thumbing the eye of rival landed gentry as it was about catching fish. There is always a clandestine mood when crossing private property to fly-fish, but this really did feel like infiltrating enemy lines. I started looking for the sheriff again—or a rancher riding a four-wheeler and waving a shotgun.

The Benson Road parallels Mink Creek almost all the way up to the headwaters. I caught glimpses of fish feeding in the creek but couldn't look away from the deplorable road for long. Barber had once called this road poor, but the mere use of the word *road* struck me as a slanderous indignity to actual roads. Even *jeep trail* seemed overly generous. The grades were precarious, and there was no room to pull over or turn around. The way was riven by erosion and studded with craggy boulders the size of microwave ovens.

We jostled along. Keller spotted deer and regaled me with regional mythology. He told me about the "old yellow schoolhouse," a quaint little brick edifice perched picturesquely on a bluff overlooking the highway, which had been Mink Creek's sole source of pedagogy during the Great Depression, when his father was a child.

"Dad used to tell the story of the day it caught on fire," said Keller. "All the girls were screaming, 'Put it out! Put it out!' and all the boys were shouting, 'Let 'er burn! Let 'er burn!'" I laughed.

"There's a Mink Creek Ghost too," he said, gesturing at another hillside. "The house isn't too far from here."

"Oh, this I gotta hear," I said.

"Well," he said, "story goes there was a pioneer couple came over here in the 1860s, came over from the old country—probably Denmark—came over on a boat, came across the plains, the whole Mormon immigration experience. And they hated it." I laughed some more.

"So, they're like, 'Let's get out of this shithole,' and they packed up to head back to the motherland."

We rolled up on a particularly rotten section of trail. I slowed down, and Keller paused his storytelling. The truck tilted alarmingly, and the suspension clattered and croaked as I eased over the boulders and gullies. This happened several times—Keller paused the story while I gritted my teeth to negotiate a dicey spot and then took up where he'd left off as we passed by.

"Story goes they'd packed up to go when suddenly the people they'd sold their house to decided to kill 'em instead of paying."

"Bit harsh."

"Yeah, well, the murderers moved in, and they had a young girl—a daughter or something—and every night she was attacked by something in her bedroom. She got these bite marks all over her. So, the Mink Creek elders go over and gave her a blessing, did an exorcism, but this thing kept attacking her."

I steered gingerly into a trail section that only just accommodated the truck. On one side were escarpments of basalt and old junipers with trunks three feet across. On the other side was a fence of stout wooden posts and taut barbed wire. The clearance to either side was the matter of a handspan. Both side mirrors had been forcibly folded back and scrub oak branches screeched terribly against the roof and fenders. When the way opened up again, Keller continued.

"One night, emboldened I guess by some neighboring ranchers, the father confronts the ghost—says, 'Come on! Leave 'er alone! I'll take y'on!' And so, it comes after him and whips his ass and leaves bite marks all over him!" We both laughed.

A variant account includes an attempt to burn down the house, but it wouldn't catch fire. On certain nights to this day, locals say, the shrieking lament of a woman can be heard on the downcanyon winds.

My truck couldn't go much faster than walking speed as it scaled the disastrous road, and there were four more private gates. We halted, swung open a gate, rolled through, closed the gate and proceeded. It was slow going. Fortunately, Keller was a gifted raconteur—the other reason I liked fishing with him. Life is too short to fish with someone who can't tell a decent story.

"You know," mused Keller as we were bucked from our seats again, "these assholes let this road go to hell so that no one can make it up here."

"But this is a public right-of-way, right?" I asked. "They can't call the sheriff on us, can they?"

"Oh," said Keller with diabolical glee, "I'd love it if they tried."

In late summer of 2006, the county commission decided in favor of public access, just as it had several times already.

"At this point" stated county attorney Todd Garbett, "we believe people historically have used this road to gain access to [Forest Service] ground, and if that can be shown, then a public right-of-way has been established."

Barber was told to cease locking gates and posting prohibitive signage, but that wasn't the end of it.

Keller scoffed. "Yeah, he probably left it unlocked for a little while, but he locked it again, and I'm not talking some little dinky padlock. This time it was one of those that weighs like five pounds."

Reluctant to take sides, the county didn't force Barber to unlock his gate, but neither did it pursue trespassing charges along the Benson Road. So, residents simply climbed over Barber's gate. Some even got their vehicles around it by laying down a section of the wire fence, driving through and then standing it back up. Keller speculated archly about how the old man must have fumed as he watched Mink Creek residents repeatedly and flagrantly exercising their right of way. It's rumored that on at least one occasion, Barber sent hired men to escort the Visigoths off the Benson Road at gunpoint. So, the conflict simmered for years in a series of spiteful skirmishes.

Then, in April 2014, Leness Keller passed away days shy of his eighty-sixth birthday. Keller and his father saw the world very differently, and they didn't always get along. Still, whenever Keller speaks of his father, there is a tone of respect that borders on reverence. I attended Leness's funeral, and it looked to me as if the entirety of southeastern Idaho had turned out to pay their respects, but Keller hinted it was no coincidence that Allen Barber lawyered up not even one month later and again petitioned Franklin County to abandon the Benson Road.

Area residents packed the county courthouse to throw back Barber's new attack. Keller's brothers, cousins and fellow sportsmen marshalled to testify, and a search got underway for deeds and maps to prove the Benson Road was a long-established public right-of-way. Keller said that's when many of the relevant documents apparently became suddenly and suspiciously scarce.

"We'd go to the Forest Service to get some map, but it'd just so happen to be missing," jeered Keller. "So we'd look up some other historic map, and it was mysteriously missing, too. Barber's people said: 'Welp, there's no maps showing it's a public right-of-way, so, that's it.'"

But so many people attended one particular meeting that the crowd was moved to a larger room in the courthouse basement. This development proved pivotal.

"We get to the bigger room," explained Keller, "and there's this big county map from the 1800s hanging on the wall, and my brother points to it, says, 'There's a map right there that shows it's a right-of-way!' Barber's people say, 'Yeah, but that's just hand-drawn!' and my brother says, 'All maps back then were hand-drawn!'"

I never met Allen Barber. I don't know if he pilfered archival maps or enlisted hired guns to enforce his will. He probably just wanted privacy. But I do know that it must have been all but impossible for Keller and other Mink Creekers to see him as anything but a dirty carpetbagger.

"Used to be pretty much everything up here was owned by a handful of families," said Keller in a wistful tone. "Used to be we all pretty much got along."

I don't know about that, either. People pay handsomely for land and guard it jealously when it's bequeathed to them. Private property rights are a cornerstone of Western civilization, but the right to access public lands is deeply compelling, too, one of the strongest threads in the cultural fabric of the American West. And it must never be forgotten that European settlers displaced indigenous people before any of these contemporary conflicts arose. The entire matter is not unlike a drive up the old Benson Road itself—immovable and treacherous obstructions to either side and a rocky, perilous way forward.

It must have scalded Mink Creek natives to watch interlopers buy up the land their forefathers once held, hunted and fished and then see it shut behind padlocks and lawyers. It could not have been unpleasant for Keller when they beat the carpetbagger back yet again. In July 2015, Franklin County again denied the Benson Road closure. This time, in addition to hearing from dozens of locals, the commission had hired a historian from Boise and a legal firm specializing in private property conflicts.

"After taking all these things into account," stated county commissioner Scott Workman, "we voted to keep the road open to the public."

It was the fifth time in twelve years that the Franklin County Commission had arrived at the same decision regarding the same petition.

I could sense the bullheadedness with which Barber and other landowners received the ruling in the way they built new fencing so close to the Benson Road. It was evident in the ridiculous frequency of their no trespassing signs—every ten feet in some places.

Keller was probably right about the deliberate neglect of the Benson Road. Whatever it might once have been—cow trail or logging road—it was no longer suitable for vehicle traffic. My old Tacoma did all right, but any truck built in the last five years would have the devil of a time squeezing through. A week later, I phoned up Franklin County commissioner Robert Swainston. The late war over the Benson Road was fought before his time in office, but I asked him, "How come Franklin County doesn't repair and maintain the Benson Road?"

"That road doesn't get used enough to justify the funds it would take to maintain it," said Swainston, "just like hundreds of miles of other unmaintained county roads."

It took Keller and me an hour to cover the three miles of Benson Road to the Forest Service boundary. There we emerged onto the public land and into a wide, welcoming sea of wild, waving grass. It looked a lot like wheat, almost waist-high and glowing in the sunshine of a waning summer. At the far end of the meadow, a pair of doe deer watched us clear the final gate and then slipped into a brake of juniper.

A half-mile later, the Benson Road vanished among the grass and aspens. Keller strolled the creek bank, scanning his erstwhile birthright. Dragonflies, dusty-gray caddisflies and vaulting hoppers filled the air. The day was hot, but a wind blew in from that place where summer contends with autumn. The scrub oak leaves were turning orange.

"I think I'll come up here for the deer hunt this year," Keller announced with a nod.

Hunting season was fast approaching. You could feel it. But Keller wasn't scouting, not really. He was recollecting.

Keller pointed and said, "Shot a deer off that ridgeline and dragged him all the way down that godforsaken road." Then he added, "Course, I was a teenager then."

Keller's stories had turned mostly to the topic of hunting, and most involved his father. "We came up here one time to hunt the Steeps—me and Dad and my brother. I'd come up early that morning, and I was waiting for them on that cliff right there, or maybe that one, but then I realized they'd

Mink Creek.

ditched me, crossed underneath me. Oh, I was pissed. So I come blazing down this way and start heading home."

He pointed at the far-off hills, retracing his route. "As I'm heading back, I see this line of bucks coming down the ridge right there. Nice ones, but I don't have time to get any closer to them, so I open up on 'em, but I've got no chance of hitting anything—they're like three hundred yards away—so I'm going blam, blam, blam, and they just keep coming." Keller fired a pantomime rifle.

"Didn't hit a single one?" I asked. "Like not even by accident?"

Keller grinned and held up an index finger. "I get down to my last shot, and I finally drop one. A three-point."

He could single out any hilltop, creek bend or wrinkle in the mountain and tell about it—a ghost story for every piece of terrain.

At last, I waded into Mink Creek. The cool, swift water cascaded over my sandals. I covered the nearest favorable water with a caddis pattern and instantly hooked a twelve-inch brookie. The variegations on his back were small and fine. His belly was bright yellow like a banana in the sun, and his head was as dusky as a grape.

As I unhooked the fish, I realized Keller hadn't even brought his flyrod. When I mentioned it, he shrugged and watched me fish, delighted that we'd finally made it to the upper Mink, delighted that the fish were amenable. I caught a couple dozen more before we hiked back to the truck, but I've already remarked on that.

Keller said Allen Barber moved out of Mink Creek shortly after the County Commission's 2015 decision, but if history serves as any lesson about the future, the fighting is overdue to erupt again. As of that September evening in 2018, the Benson Road was still open, if nearly impassable. I can't say if it's open today or will be tomorrow.

As we got in the truck to drive back, I said to Keller, "You grew up down in town, but this right here was basically your family's backyard."

"Oh, definitely," said Keller, nodding soberly. "Actually, not even that," he added, scanning the hills again. "This was our home. This is where we really lived."

ABOUT THE AUTHOR

Chadd VanZanten is an outdoor writer and the author of numerous works on fly-fishing and backpacking. His book *On Fly-Fishing the Wind River Range* was named 2019–2020 Book of the Year by the League of Utah Writers. When he is not writing, he is fishing. The opposite is also true.